Extended reviews

There is now widespread recognition that "lifestyle treatment" (appropriate diet and physical activity) is as, if not more, important than drug treatment for many people with conditions such as diabetes, heart disease, high cholesterol and high blood pressure. The same healthy lifestyle advice is not only appropriate for the great majority of people with these conditions, but it is also the best way of preventing them and avoiding overweight and obesity which are important risk factors for many chronic diseases.

Many people want to make the necessary changes, but lack the culinary skills to produce tasty and healthy meals. This book contains a substantial number of delicious recipes which will hel⋯⋯⋯⋯⋯⋯⋯⋯⋯⋯⋯⋯⋯⋯⋯⋯⋯⋯⋯⋯⋯⋯⋯⋯⋯for every occasion.

Jim
Pro⋯⋯⋯⋯⋯⋯⋯⋯⋯⋯ ty of Otago
Dir⋯⋯⋯⋯⋯⋯⋯⋯⋯⋯ esearch

CW00925047

So many people are interested in improving their health but feel that they don't know where to begin; that so much advice is contradictory. This book illustrates that key foods such as fruit and vegetables, fish and fibre rich foods such as wholegrains and legumes will be beneficial in preventing or managing a number of chronic conditions.

Many also delay adopting a healthier style of eating because of the fear that it will be boring and that they will miss out on so many interesting flavours. Julie has assembled a range of recipes for all situations that are major on flavour and colour. Her introductions and methods encourage attractive and innovative presentations that keep the interest factor high.

Teresa Cleary
NZ Registered Dietitian, Diabetes Auckland

References

This list is not comprehensive of all the books, medical journals and documents used in developing NOSH. It includes the more significant ones.

1   New Zealand Guidelines Group (2003). Evidence Based Best Practice Guideline: Management of Type 2 Diabetes.

2   New Zealand Guidelines Group, National Heart Foundation, Stroke Foundation of New Zealand (2003). Evidence Based Best Practice Guideline: Assessment & Management of Cardiovascular Risk.

3   Brand – Miller J Prof & Foster-Powell (2005). The New Glucose Revolution Shopper's Guide to GI Values 2005 (Australia and New Zealand). Hodder.

4   PriceWaterhouseCoopers (2001). Type 2 Diabetes: Managing for Better Outcomes. A report for Diabetes New Zealand Inc.

5   Mann JI, De Leeuw I, Hermansen K et al (2004). Evidence-based nutritional approaches to the treatment and prevention of diabetes mellitus. Nutr Metab Cardiovasc Dis 14: 373–394.

6   Ministry of Health (2003). Food and Nutrition Guidelines for Healthy Adults: A background paper. Wellington.

7   Ministry of Health and the University of Auckland (2003). Nutrition and the Burden of Disease: 1997 – 2011. Wellington.

8   Ministry of Health (2004). Tracking the Obesity Epidemic: New Zealand 1997 - 2011. Wellington.

9   Ministry of Health (2003). Healthy Eating - Healthy Action. A background 2003. Wellington.

10 WHO/FAO Expert Consultation (2003). Diet, Nutrition and the Prevention of Chronic Diseases – WHO Technical Report Series 916. Geneva.

11 Alexander Stephanie (2004). The Cook's Companion. The complete book of ingredients and recipes for the Australian kitchen. Lantern. Penguin Books.

12 McGee Harold (2004). McGee on Food & Cooking: an encyclopedia of kitchen science history and culture. Hodder & Stoughton. London.

13 New Zealands Guild of Foodwriters (1999). Handbook (2nd edition).

NOSH

delicious & responsible eating

by registered dietitian **Julie Leeper**
photography by Gareth Leeper

delicious & responsible eating

NOSH

PRE DIABETES **DIABETES** HEART DISEASE **CHOLESTEROL** HEALTHY WEIGHT **HEALTHY EATING**

PRESSURE **CARDIOPROTECTIVE DIET** PRE-DIABETES **DIABETES HEART DISEASE** CHOLESTEROL

Author: Julie Leeper (nee Stockdill) – Recipe development and nutrition information
BCApSC, PGDipDiet (1994), NZRD, Cert Adult Teaching

Food Photography: Gareth Leeper
Food Stylist: Julie Leeper
Food Props: Ballantynes Ltd, Christchurch, New Zealand
Peer Reviewers: Jim Mann, Professor in Human Nutrition and Medicine, University
of Otago, and Director of the Edgar National Centre for Diabetes Research, Dunedin,
New Zealand
Teresa Cleary, NZ Registered Dietitian, Diabetes Auckland, New Zealand
Graphic Design: Tonic Design Ltd
Printer: PMP Print Ltd

© NOSH, Julie Leeper 2006
All rights reserved. No part of this publication may be reproduced or transmitted
in any form or by any means, electronic or mechanical, including photocopying,
recording, or any information storage and retrieval system, without permission in
writing from the author.

Although every effort has been made to ensure the accuracy of information, NOSH
shall accept no liability, for loss or damage, to any person or entity, caused or alleged
to be caused, directly or indirectly, by the information contained in this book.
This publication is intended to provide generalised information only and not to render
professional advice. Any person with a medical condition or health issue of any sort
should first seek the advice of a registered health professional.

ISBN-13: 978-0-473-11393-3
ISBN-10: 0-473-11393-7

contents

Welcome to Nosh

At last a recipe book that caters for people with a number of different dietary conditions such as diabetes, impaired glucose tolerance, pre–diabetes, high cholesterol, high blood pressure and weight loss. Better still, it's also suitable for those who just simply want to eat healthy, or want to incorporate the glycaemic index into their diet. No, we haven't taken everything out of the recipes to cater for all these medical conditions, but rather, they all have very similar dietary requirements – that is healthy eating.

NOSH contains a mix of traditional and contemporary recipes, so there are recipes to suit everyone. NOSH is not just about producing healthy food, but food that is also tasty and visually appealing. Our taste testers ranged in age, socioeconomic status, culture and food preferences. The biggest critic was myself!

As a result of client feedback, NOSH recipes have been developed mainly for 2 or 4 people. However, some recipes have larger serves due to the impractical nature of making smaller quantities. In many instances the extra serves will freeze well.

NOSH recipes have not had all the fat, sugar and salt removed and low fibre ingredients substituted fully with high fibre ones. Some fat, sugar, salt and low fibre ingredients are essential for flavour, colour and texture. We have cut back not cut out! Just because these recipes are healthier, is not a licence to eat more of them! If you have never eaten baked products and desserts frequently, then don't start. Rather, keep them as occasional eats. Don't forget that you can gain weight by eating too much healthy food!!! Portion size does matter.

Sometimes recipes claim to be healthy just because they are reduced in fat. Healthy recipes should not only be low in fat but, any fat included should be of a healthier type. They should also contain only small amounts of sugar and salt and include some form of fibre.

NOSH recipes have been made healthy by:
- Keeping the total amount of fat, particularly saturated fat low
- Using only small amounts of sugar and using fruit as a natural sweetener
- Using small amounts of lean meat
- Incorporating legumes
- Incorporating fish into recipes
- Including fibre, both soluble and insoluble
- Incorporating a variety of different coloured fruit and vegetables, where possible
- Adding small amounts of nuts and seeds
- Using herbs and spices for flavouring instead of fat, sugar and salt
- Including low glycaemic index ingredients where possible.

NOSH is not a nutrition book but rather a recipe book that translates science into practice. NOSH is only able to give generalised nutrition advice and information. For nutrition information specific to your individual needs, talk to a dietitian.

Julie Leeper
NZ Registered Dietitian

Recipe Information

Important information about NOSH recipes

Recipes that are low in fat and sugar, and high in fibre, are more difficult to produce successfully. This is when accurate measuring of ingredients, using correct mixing techniques, the right oven temperature and tin or dish size becomes very important. This is particularly so for baked products and desserts.

Measures

Use measuring spoons and cups. Measures are level unless otherwise indicated. The following standard New Zealand metric measurements are used:

Cup

¼ cup = 60 ml	⅓ cup = 80 ml
½ cup = 125 ml	1 cup = 250 ml

Spoons

¼ teaspoon = 1.25 ml	½ teaspoon = 2.5 ml
1 teaspoon = 5 ml	1 dessertspoon = 10 ml
1 tablespoon = 15 ml	

Abbreviations of measures

t = teaspoon	D = dessertspoon
T = tablespoon	C = cup
cm = centimetres	ml = millilitres
l = litres	g = grams
kg = kilograms	°C = degrees Celsius

Ingredients

Use the ingredients as specified in the recipe. Substituting or leaving ingredients out may affect the look, texture, flavour and nutritional value of the product.

(i) Baking Powder: Some of the baking recipes use larger amounts of baking powder than normal. High fibre ingredients often make products heavy and dense so a way of compensating is to use more baking powder.

(ii) Eggs: Medium eggs are size 6 unless otherwise stated.

(iii) Salt: Most of the recipes do not add salt as they already contain some ingredients that are salty.

(iv) Sweeteners & Sugar: A small amount of sugar is an acceptable part of a healthy diet for everyone, including people with Diabetes. A small amount of sugar, in NOSH recipes, has been included to produce a better tasting, looking and textured product. Where larger quantities of sweetening are required, this will be stated in the following way:

sugar^S or equivalent sweetener^{ES}

S = For the measure given, you can choose to use sugar, or an equivalent sweetener, if you have:
• a healthy body shape and weight
• normal triglyceride levels and are lean
• Diabetes and are lean, active and have well controlled blood glucose levels

ES = For the measure given, an equivalent low calorie sweetener is a better choice if you have:
• excess body weight
• high triglyceride levels
• Diabetes, and are also overweight
• Diabetes, and have high or unstable blood glucose levels

What sweetener to use: In some of the recipes, NOSH specifies the sweetener. Where it isn't specified and the sweetener is to be cooked, use a suitable low calorie sweetener that doesn't lose its sweetness with heat such as: granular Splenda®, liquid Sucaryl or Sucromax or a reduced calorie sweetener such as Denta Sweet™ (Xylitol). Granular Equal™ is best added at the end of cooking or in recipes that have been specially developed using Equal™.

PLEASE NOTE: The following sweeteners are safe to use during pregnancy and for children who are 2 years or younger: Splenda®, Equal™ and Denta Sweet™.

How much sweetener to use: Some sweeteners are very sweet, particularly liquid varieties. Therefore you only need to use small amounts to get the equivalent sweetness of sugar. To determine how much sweetener to use, check the conversion factors on the containers. These may change from time to time. Always measure in spoons or cups – never weigh sweeteners as they are mostly lighter than sugar.

(v) Gluten Free

NOSH is not a gluten free recipe book however it does contain some gluten free recipes. These have been highlighted, as some people may have the dietary conditions stated in this book and also be on a gluten free diet. Gluten free means that the food must contain no detectable gluten, oats or malt. (FSANZ Food Standards Code: Standard 1.2.8). The following symbol, which can be found underneath the nutrition information, is used to indicate gluten free recipes:

GF* = Gluten Free

The recipe is gluten free or it can be made gluten free with some modifications, as listed. Check spices and dried herbs to make sure they are gluten free – in their pure form they will be, but sometimes anti–caking or carriers are added which may contain gluten. When choosing gluten free ingredients read the labels on packaged foods or consult the Gluten Free Commercial Food List: www.mfd.co.nz

(vi) GI = Glycaemic Index

This is a ranking based on the food's effect on blood glucose levels. Recipes in NOSH are ranked low, medium or high. They have been calculated using average GI values.

GI: Low Foods with a low GI, cause a smaller and more gradual rise in blood glucose levels.
GI: Moderate Foods with a moderate GI, cause blood glucose levels to rise moderately.
GI: High Foods with a high GI, cause blood glucose levels to rise more quickly and to a higher level.

Low GI foods help with weight loss and better management of blood glucose levels. High GI foods give a quick burst of energy which is beneficial for some sports. See page 19 for more information on the Glycaemic Index.

Methods

When combining ingredients, gentle mixing by hand and not with a cake mixer, is recommended unless otherwise stated. Over mixing will make products tough and may cause muffins to peak and cakes and loaves to crack.

Tips:
- Sift dry ingredients where possible.
- Beat egg whites until thick and foamy and not until stiff and dry. Fold them through the mixture, gently.
- Keep mixtures wet as this will help create a more moist and lighter product.

Tins and Dishes

Tin and dish sizes affect the look of a product and the cooking time.
Tips:
- Use tin and dish sizes as specified.
- Always grease or line tins or dishes unless otherwise indicated.

Cooking Temperatures

Oven temperatures are given, in degrees Celcius (°C), for fan forced and standard ovens. NOSH recipes have been trialled using a fan forced oven. If using a standard oven, cooking times may need to be adjusted.
Tips:
- Oven temperatures should be reached before cooking.
- Oven temperatures and cooking times will vary from oven to oven.

Storage & Keeping Qualities

Reduced fat and/or sugar products will not keep as long as products that have more fat and sugar in them.
Tips:
- Store baked products, in airtight containers in the refrigerator.
- The baked products are best eaten fresh. Products such as muffins and scones can be successfully frozen and reheated in a microwave.
- Preserves should be placed in sterilised jars, sealed and stored in the refrigerator. Care should be taken when using these to ensure that clean, uncontaminated utensils are used.

Nutritional Analysis Information

Each recipe has been computer analysed using Foodworks.™ The nutritional information is relevant to the serving size as stated by the analysis. Increasing the number of servings (making the serving smaller) will decrease all the figures. Decreasing the number of servings (making the servings bigger) will increase the figures. Where there is an option to use sugar or an equivalent sweetener, the analysis is calculated using a sweetener. If sugar is used, there would be an increase in kilojoules, calories and carbohydrate. Detailed information about nutrients, and their recommended amounts, are given in pages 10 – 13.

Ingredients

With fat and sugar at a minimum it is important to use good quality ingredients where possible. Many NOSH recipes use quite a number of ingredients. This is necessary to achieve products which have a desirable texture, taste and appearance. Deleting or even substituting ingredients may affect the overall product. Most of the recipes contain ingredients that are common and readily available. The recipes can be adjusted for flavour. If the flavours are too strong, then cut back on the spices and herbs, or for more flavour add more. Adjusting spices and herbs will not affect the overall nutritional value of the recipe unless they are accompanied with fat, sugar or salt.

Fat and Cholesterol

Some fat in the diet is essential for good health. However, too much fat is undesirable. Fat provides a concentrated form of energy, containing twice the amount of kilojoules (calories) per gram than carbohydrate and protein. As a high fat diet increases the risk of obesity, heart disease, type 2 diabetes and some cancers, most adults should be eating a low fat diet (50 – 80 grams per day depending on their energy requirements), even though they may have a healthy weight. For those who are overweight an intake of fat less than 50 grams per day should be encouraged to assist with weight loss.

There are 3 main types of fat – saturated, monounsaturated and polyunsaturated (see Table 1). Saturated fats are found predominantly in animal based foods but coconut, chocolate and palm oil also contain saturated fat. Most saturated fats raise blood cholesterol levels and therefore these fats should be kept to a minimum in the diet.

Unsaturated fats (monounsaturated and polyunsaturated) are found predominantly in plant and sea foods. These fats do not increase blood cholesterol levels. If saturated fats are replaced with unsaturated fats then a beneficial effect on blood cholesterol levels will be seen. Omega 3 fats (see Table 1), a polyunsaturated fat, should be included regularly in the diet as they can reduce heart and blood vessel disease risk. To help achieve recommended levels, of omega 3 fats, oily fish should be eaten at least two times a week. Also include, in your diet, plant sources that are high in omega 3 fats, such as walnuts, sunflower seeds, linseed and canola based margarines or oils.

Cholesterol is found only in animal foods (see Table 1). As it can increase blood cholesterol levels, in some people, it should be restricted to less than 300 mg per day or less if blood cholesterol levels are already raised.

Table 1: Fats and Cholesterol in Foods

	Saturated Fats	Polyunsaturated Fats	Monounsaturated Fats
Spreads	Butter, semi–soft butter, butter blends, shortenings	Sunflower & safflower based margarines, Proactiv™ spread	Canola,* olive & avocado based margarines, Logical spread™
Oils and Fat	Lard, suet, dripping, palm & coconut oils, solid baking margarines, hard vegetable fats (i.e: copha)	Sunflower, safflower, soybean, sesame, grapeseed, linseed/flaxseed,* wheatgerm oils	Canola,* olive, avocado, peanut oils
Nuts and Seeds	Coconut	Walnuts,* brazil & pine nuts Pumpkin, sunflower, sesame & linseeds*	Peanuts, hazelnuts, almonds, cashews, pistachios, pecans, macadamia nuts
Other	Meat fat, chicken skin & fat, pate, coconut cream, chocolate, cream, cheese, sourcream/cream cheese	Salmon,* tuna,* sardines,* kahawai,* trevally,* kingfish,* warehou,* dory,* mussels,* oysters,* eel*	Olives, avocado
Cholesterol	Egg yolks, brains, liver, kidney, meat fat, prawns, fish roe, squid, cream, butter, cheese		*Good Source of Omega–3's

Fat adds flavour to foods and affects the texture of products making them tender and moist. Fat tends to mute sweetness so when reducing fat in recipes, less sweetness is required. In NOSH, fats that are predominantly unsaturated, such as soft margarines and oil, are used in place of butter. The use of cocoa, chocolate and coconut is limited. Higher fat dairy products are substituted with lower fat varieties. Small amounts of lean meat or skinned poultry are used and legumes are sometimes added to meat dishes to extend them. The use of egg yolks are limited in order to reduce the amount of saturated fat and cholesterol. Deep frying is avoided and if frying is required, then a non–stick frying pan, or an ordinary pan smeared with a small amount of oil or cooking spray is used.

With less fat in the recipes, other ingredients have been included to improve the texture and taste of products. Yoghurt and buttermilk help tenderise, add moistness and create a more velvet like texture in products. Additional liquid adds moistness and egg whites add volume and lightness to products. Spices and herbs help replace the loss of flavour when reducing fat.

Salt

Eating too much salt (sodium chloride) or dietary sodium can increase blood pressure levels. In the New Zealand diet, the major proportion of salt comes from processed foods and a smaller amount is added during cooking or at the table. For the general adult population the recommended amount of sodium ranges from 920 – 2300 mg per day. This equates to one teaspoon of salt, maximum, per day.

Salt is used in products for flavour and is important in yeast doughs to improve the texture. NOSH uses only small amounts of salt or salty ingredients and utilises herbs and spices to enhance flavour. If you are used to eating more salt then you may well notice the difference. You can, over time, train your taste buds to appreciate food with less salt. The best way to do this is to gradually cut back the amount of salt you use. Try to use salt only once – either in cooking or at the table. Where salt is used, it should be iodised, to avoid mild iodine deficiencies and goitre.

Carbohydrates & Fibre

Carbohydrate foods should make up the bulk of the diet. They are broken down during digestion to glucose which provides fuel for the body. Foods rich in carbohydrate are breads, cereals, pasta, rice, fruit, starchy vegetables, legumes and sugars. Carbohydrate foods should supply the most energy in our diet. The exact amount of carbohydrate that you need depends on factors such as your weight, age and level of activity. Most adults should be eating at least 6 servings of breads, cereals and starchy vegetables each day. An example of a serving is: 1 slice of bread or ½ cup of cooked pasta or ⅓ cup of muesli or 1 small potato.

Eating carbohydrate foods, which are also high in fibre, is preferable. There are two main types of fibre – soluble and insoluble (see Table 2). Insoluble fibre is important for bowel health. Both insoluble and soluble fibre help with weight management as fibre is filling and tends to satisfy for longer. Soluble fibre also helps reduce blood glucose levels after meals and can help reduce blood cholesterol levels. For the general adult population 25 – 30 grams per day of fibre is recommended. People with raised blood cholesterol levels should aim for at least 30 grams of fibre per day, and people with diabetes, 40 grams or more, with half of that being soluble. Diets that also contain a proportion of carbohydrate foods that have a low glycaemic index (GI) have been shown to lower blood glucose and lipid levels and reduce weight. For more information on the GI see information on low GI diets (page 19).

Table 2: Types of Fibre

Soluble Fibre	Insoluble Fibre
Oats, barley, wheatgerm, rice bran Legumes (lentils, beans etc) Apple, citrus fruit, prunes, raisins, sultanas	Wholegrains, wheat bran, wholemeal flour Vegetables Fruits with edible seeds (strawberries)

The addition of fibre to foods alters the texture, colour and flavour of products. In NOSH, the recipes include fibre containing foods such as fruit or vegetables, nuts, legumes and or some form of bran. Often oat bran is incorporated in recipes due to it being soluble in nature. It also has a tenderising and moisturising effect on baked goods. Where possible the skins of fruits, vegetables and nuts should be left on as this will provide extra fibre. In baking recipes not all of the white flour is replaced with wholemeal flour or bran as this would produce a product that would not be very palatable. Rather a mix of half and half is often used. To compensate for the extra fibre, extra liquid is necessary and is why many NOSH baking recipes are more liquid than standard recipes. High fibre ingredients can make products rather heavy and the texture dense. Extra baking powder, and the use of beaten egg whites help counteract some of these effects.

Sugar & Sweeteners

There are a number of different sugars found in foods. The commonly known ones are glucose (syrups, honey, fruit), fructose (fruit), lactose (milk products), and sucrose (table sugar). Sucrose, which is commonly added to foods, provides concentrated energy (kilojoules) and no other nutritive value (vitamins/minerals/fibre) in the diet. For these reasons, sucrose should only be eaten in relatively small amounts, even for those people who are lean, active, have normal blood cholesterol levels and no diabetes. For people who are overweight, or who have high triglyceride levels or diabetes, smaller amounts of sucrose are permissible. As a guide, this would be about 1 – 2 tablespoons per day. As sucrose has been shown only to have a moderate effect on blood glucose levels, people with diabetes do not need to totally avoid it. However, it is best incorporated as part of a high fibre snack or part of a meal.

Sugar has a number of roles in foods. It affects the texture, tenderness, moistness, flavour and colour of products. Foods without sugar tend to look pale and unappetising. The use of some sugar in NOSH recipes is to produce better looking, tasting and textured products. To produce crisp biscuits some sugar is necessary. Keeping them thin and cooking them for longer will contribute towards making them crisper. Tenderness and moistness issues are discussed under the fat section.

In NOSH some of the sugar is replaced with fruit (fresh, dried, cooked, juice) and is often topped up with mainly small amounts of a low calorie sweetener to provide enough sweetness. Much controversy surrounds some of the low calorie sweeteners, however research shows that they are safe to consume in limited amounts with the exception of some sweeteners during pregnancy and in the first two years of life. The advantage of low calorie sweeteners are that they provide sweetness with less or no kilojoules. The downside is that they do not replace the other properties of sugar such as crispness, browning and tenderising. Most of the baking and dessert recipes in NOSH that require a low calorie sweetener, use granular Splenda®, which is made from sugar but is altered to not affect blood glucose levels. It is safe to use during pregnancy.

There are a number of natural sweeteners such as xylitol, sorbitol, mannitol, isomalt, and lactitol, that occur naturally in fruits and vegetables. These contain fewer kilojoules than sugar but more than the low calorie sweeteners. Xylitol, which is marketed as Dentasweet™ by Annies, is available from some supermarkets and pharmacies or through Annies website (www.annies.co.nz). NOSH recipes have not been developed using this sweetener. However, it can be used in place of the sugar and Splenda®. Xylitol may affect blood glucose levels, but this will be minimal. It may cause some stomach discomfort if consumed in large quantities.

Some sweeteners are very sweet so it is best to add small amounts to start with, then add, to taste. Low calorie sweeteners tend to have an after taste – some people are more sensitive to this than others. The after taste is more evident if a product is over sweetened. Where possible add sweeteners at the end of cooking to avoid them producing a bitter taste.

Nutrition for Health

Good nutrition is essential for health. Inappropriate nutrition is linked to a number of medical conditions such as obesity, type 2 diabetes, pre–diabetes, heart disease, high blood pressure, strokes, cancer and osteoporosis. In New Zealand it has been estimated that poor nutrition and inactivity are responsible for more than 40% of deaths. Even small improvements in nutrition and physical activity levels can have considerable benefits on overall health.

Healthy Eating for all

Many people believe that prevention is better than cure but few practice it. Often dietary changes are not made until a medical condition, requiring changes in eating habits, is diagnosed. Healthy eating has many beneficial effects. It can help lower blood glucose levels, blood pressure, blood cholesterol and weight and improve mental and physical well–being. Healthy eating is not just for people with diabetes, heart disease and those that are overweight but rather it is something that we all should be doing. Healthy eating does not exclude foods but includes foods in the right quantities and frequencies. The following New Zealand Dietary Guidelines for Healthy Adults, in Table 3, have been developed based on research and provide a guide for a healthy lifestyle:

Table 3: The New Zealand Dietary Guidelines for Healthy Adults

1 Maintain a healthy body weight by eating well and by daily physical activity.
2 Eat well by including a variety of nutritious foods from each of the 4 major food groups each day:
·eat plenty of vegetables and fruit.
·eat plenty of breads and cereals, preferably wholegrain varieties.
·have milk and milk products in the diet, preferably reduced or low fat options.
·include lean meat, poultry, seafood, eggs or alternatives.
3 Prepare foods or choose pre–pared foods, drinks and snacks:
·with minimal added fat, especially saturated fat.
·that are low in salt. If using salt, choose iodised salt.
·with little added sugar. Limit your intake of high sugar foods.
4 Drink plenty of liquids each day, especially water.
5 If choosing to drink alcohol, limit your intake.
6 Purchase, prepare, cook and store food to ensure food safety.

NZ Ministry of Health, 2000

NOSH recipes are suitable for those choosing to follow a healthy lifestyle as they include a variety of nutritious foods and generally contain small amounts of fat, particularly saturated fat, salt and sugar. Being lower in kilojoules than standard recipes, they will help achieve and maintain a healthy weight.

Preventing Heart Disease

In New Zealand, 40% of deaths are a result of cardiovascular disease (CVD). Heart attacks, angina and transient ischemic attacks are all forms of CVD. CVD is usually the result of a blood clot forming on fatty deposits (plaques) on the walls of major blood vessels (arteries). Factors (often known as risk factors) that increase the likelihood of developing CVD are age, gender, ethnicity, family history, pre–diabetes, diabetes, raised blood pressure, raised blood lipids, smoking, unhealthy diet, physical inactivity and obesity. The lifestyle factors that can be changed are discussed below.

Preventing Heart Disease – Eating a Cardioprotective Diet

Everyone, even those with a low CVD risk, should be encouraged to adopt a cardioprotective diet as this will reduce their risk of developing CVD. A cardioprotective diet is healthy eating with an emphasis on particular substances in food, such as dietary fibre, antioxidants and polyunsaturated fats, that delay the onset of CVD.

The five food groups that contribute protective substances and the recommended servings* are…
· **Fruit:** at least 3 serves a day and
  Vegetables: at least 3 – 4 serves a day, particularly coloured types
· **Breads and Cereals:** at least 6 serves a day, particularly wholegrain varieties
· **Fatty Fish and Seafood:** 1 – 2 serves a week and
  Legumes: 4 – 5 serves a week
· **Low Fat Milk, Soy and Milk Products:** 2 – 3 serves a day
· **Oils and Spreads:** 3 serves or more a day, plant based and excluding palm and coconut

*For information on serving sizes, search for the food table, on the following website **www.heartfoundation.org.nz**

The cardioprotective diet also limits foods and drinks that increase the likelihood of developing CVD, such as saturated fat, sugar, salt, alcohol and eating too much energy (kilojoules/calories). NOSH recipes are suitable for those following a cardioprotective diet as they have been based on the National Heart Foundation of New Zealand's Food Based Dietary Statements as seen in Table 4.

Table 4: The National Heart Foundation of New Zealand Food Based Dietary Statements

1   Enjoy three meals each day, select from dishes that include plant foods and fish and avoid dairy fat, meat fat or deep fried foods.
2   Choose fruits and/or vegetables at every meal and most snacks.
3   Select whole grains, whole grain breads, or high fibre breakfast cereals in place of white bread and low fibre varieties at most meals and snacks.
4   Include fish, or dried peas, beans and soy products, or a small serving of lean meat or skinned poultry, at one or two meals each day.
5   Choose low fat milk and milk products, soy or legume products every day.
6   Use small amounts of oil, margarine, nuts or seeds.
7   Drink plenty of fluids each day, particularly water, and limit sugar–sweetened drinks and alcohol.
8   Use only small amounts of total fats and oils, sugar and salt when cooking and preparing meals, snacks, or drinks. Choose ready–prepared foods low in these ingredients.
9   Mostly avoid or rarely include butter, deep–fried and fatty foods, and only occasionally choose sweet bakery products.

Preventing Heart Disease – Reducing high blood pressure (Hypertension)

Blood pressure is the measure of how hard the heart has to work to pump blood around the body. High blood pressure is dangerous as it increases the risk of having a stroke, heart attack or kidney damage. One in five New Zealanders, over 15 years of age, have high blood pressure (160/95 mmHg) or are taking medication to lower it. High blood pressure may be caused by or exacerbated by stress, lack of exercise, salt intake, being overweight and alcohol intake. Following a cardioprotective diet (see Table 4), limiting high intakes of sodium and alcohol and weight loss if overweight will help lower blood pressure levels. Physical activity is also beneficial.

Preventing Heart Disease – Reducing high blood cholesterol (Hyperlipidaemia)

Cholesterol is a white, waxy like substance that is produced in the liver. It is a normal and essential component of our bodies. However, having too much cholesterol in the blood increases the risk of having a heart attack or stroke. Raised blood cholesterol levels are common in New Zealand with at least 23% of people having levels greater than 6.5 mmol/l. Raised levels may be a result of obesity, diabetes and/or insulin resistance therefore treatment should first target these conditions.

Cholesterol medication should not be the only measure used for reducing high blood cholesterol levels. Diet has an independent and an additive effect on reducing heart disease as it not only reduces blood cholesterol levels but also improves the overall lipid profile, decreases blood pressure and reduces blood clotting. A cardioprotective diet is recommended for those with lipid abnormalities. Diets rich in soluble fibre (see Table 2) also have beneficial effects on cholesterol levels. Weight loss for those who are overweight or have excess weight around the abdominal area is also recommended.

Preventing Heart Disease – Managing other risk factors

Excess weight, especially around the stomach, increases the risk of CVD. For people who have CVD risk factors and a healthy body weight and shape it is important to prevent weight gain. For those who are overweight or have an unhealthy body shape then weight loss would be beneficial. Being smokefree and physically active (at least 30 minutes of moderate intensity activity, on most days of the week) will also reduce the risk of CVD. High blood glucose levels that are elevated for long periods will also increase the risk of CVD. If you have pre–diabetes, Type 1 or Type 2 Diabetes then aim to keep your blood glucose levels as close as possible to the normal range.

Healthy Weight & Shape

Obesity has reached epidemic levels with more than 50% of the adult population in New Zealand being overweight and 10% of school age children now obese. There are many factors responsible for obesity, however the major drivers of the epidemic are mainly due to poor diet, physical inactivity and an obesogenic environment. For most people, these factors are able to be modified.

Excess weight is linked to Type 2 Diabetes, heart disease, increased blood pressure, strokes, gallbladder disease, sleep apnoea, impaired fertility and some cancers. People who are obese are 40 times more likely to develop Type 2 Diabetes and 2 – 3 times more likely to develop cardiovascular disease. Weight loss improves cholesterol levels, blood pressure, blood glucose levels, insulin sensitivity and can delay people with impaired glucose tolerance (IGT) developing diabetes. Even small amounts of weight loss (5 – 10% of body weight) can offer benefits.

Body mass index BMI (kg/m^2) is a measure that is commonly used to determine suitable body weights. It is age independent and the same for both sexes. To determine your BMI follow steps outlined in Table 5.

Table 6: Classification of weight according to BMI (kg/m^2)

Classification	European & other	Maori & Pacific Peoples
Healthy Weight	18.5 – 24.99	18.5 – 25.99
Overweight	25.0 – 29.9	26.0 – 31.9
Obesity	30 or greater	32 or greater
Extreme Obesity	40 or greater	40 or greater

NZ Ministry of Health, 2004

Table 5: How to calculate Body Mass Index (BMI)

An example – Sue is 64 kg and 1.67 m tall

1	Measure your height in metres	1.67 m
2	Multiply your height by your height	1.67 m x 1.67 m = 2.79 m^2
3	Measure your weight in kilograms	64 kg
4	Divide your weight by the answer you got in number 2	64 kg ÷ 2.79 m^2 = 22.9 kg/m^2
5	Now compare your BMI with Table 6	22.9 = healthy weight range

BMI does not take into account where body fat is distributed. Excess abdominal fat is a better measure of the risk of developing obesity related diseases, such as type 2 diabetes and cardiovascular disease (CVD), than total body weight. Waist circumference is a simple way of measuring abdominal fat. To determine waist circumference simply measure the waist. Recommended levels are seen in Table 7. These measures are only appropriate for Caucasians. For Asian populations these levels are likely to be lower and for Maori and Pacific Island people higher.

Table 7: Effect of Waist Circumference on Obesity Related Diseases

Classification	Women	Male
Increased Risk	80 cm or more	94 cm or more
Substantially Increased Risk	88 cm or more	102 cm or more

WHO Geneva, 2000

For people who are of a healthy weight it is important to prevent weight gain through eating a healthy diet and participating in regular physical activity. For those who are overweight a reduction in energy (kilojoules/calories), a healthy diet (low fat, low sugar and high fibre) and regular physical activity is recommended in order to reduce weight. Care should be taken not to remove foods that have important nutrients like vegetables and fruit, wholegrains, breads and cereals, milk and milk products, meat, eggs and legumes. Rather, lower fat versions of these foods should be chosen. Foods high in energy and low in nutrients such as alcohol, soft drinks, chips, cakes, biscuits and sweets should be limited. A low glycaemic index (GI) diet (see page 19) can also help promote weight loss as low GI foods tend to be more filling and satisfying.

Crash or fad diets should be avoided as they only promote weight loss in the short term. They often either require avoidance of certain food groups and/or they encourage excessive amounts of foods which are not necessarily good for health. Weight loss should not be seen as a quick fix but rather the need to change ones lifestyle for ever in order to achieve and maintain a lower weight.

NOSH recipes are suitable for people trying to maintain or lose weight. For those trying to lose weight use mainly the recipes with less kilojoules in them and keep the higher kilojoule recipes for special occasions. Even though the baking and dessert recipes are mainly lower in kilojoules than their normal counterparts, these should not be eaten regularly if you are trying to lose weight.

Diabetes

In New Zealand the estimated prevalence of diagnosed diabetes is 3–4% of the population. However it is thought that for every person diagnosed with diabetes there is another that is undiagnosed.

Diabetes is a condition where there is not enough insulin produced and/or it is not working properly. Insulin is needed to keep the glucose in the blood at the right level. Too much glucose in the blood can damage the body over time causing blindness, amputations, kidney and heart problems. There are two main types of diabetes mellitus: Type 1 and Type 2. Type 1 diabetes is an autoimmune disease in which the insulin producing cells in the pancreas are destroyed. It is more commonly diagnosed in children and young adults. It is often diagnosed quickly due to the rapid onset of symptoms. People with Type 1 diabetes require insulin treatment along with dietary management and physical activity. Type 2 diabetes is more common than Type 1 diabetes with 85–90% of New Zealanders who have diabetes, having this type of diabetes. It is due to less insulin being produced and/or the insulin not being as effective. Type 2 diabetes can be present for many years before symptoms appear. It is more common in adults but is now appearing in young adolescents and children. With age, the risk of Type 2 diabetes increases. Being overweight, inactive, having a family history of diabetes, having had diabetes during pregnancy, and being of Maori, Pacific Island or Asian descent increases the likelihood of developing this disorder. Management of Type 2 diabetes is through diet and regular physical activity. Some people may also require medication.

Weight management is a major dietary goal for those with Type 2 diabetes. The aim is to prevent weight gain, attempt weight loss and/or reduce waist circumference. Reducing energy dense foods (high fat and sugar containing foods), alcohol and increasing physical activity levels will assist with weight loss. If significant weight loss does not occur through changing the types of foods eaten then a prescribed energy reduction diet may be necessary.

In regard to diet, the focus should not just be on reducing sugar but rather on gradually adopting a cardioprotective diet (see Table 4) which reduces saturated fat, added sugar and white flour products, is low in salt and alcohol, and includes wholegrains, legumes, fruit, vegetables, fish and some polyunsaturated fat.

The type and amount of carbohydrate in the diet is very important. The type of carbohydrate will determine how quickly it is broken down to glucose. The amount determines how much glucose is produced. Including carbohydrate foods that have a low to moderate glycaemic index, and are high in fibre, will help reduce high blood glucose levels following meals. Consistent amounts of carbohydrate in meals, from day to day, will enable more stable blood glucose levels.

The recipes in NOSH are suitable for people with diabetes as they have been developed on the principles of a cardioprotective diet, they include low glycaemic index and high fibre ingredients and they avoid large amounts of carbohydrate in a serving. Use the nutrition information provided with each recipe to help you obtain consistent amounts of carbohydrate in your meals.

Pre–diabetes (Impaired Glucose Tolerance and Impaired Fasting Glycaemia)

Impaired glucose tolerance (IGT) and impaired fasting glycaemia (IFG) are stages between normal blood glucose levels and diabetes. People with IGT and IFG are at risk of developing Type 2 diabetes and its associated complications. The exact prevalence of IGT and IFG in New Zealand is unknown. However, it has been estimated that more than 300,000 people have IGT. Studies have shown that the onset of diabetes can be delayed and/or prevented with healthy eating and regular physical activity. For people with IGT and IFG who are overweight, weight reduction and maintenance of weight loss is important. An adoption of a cardioprotective diet, is also appropriate due to the increased risk of developing CVD.

Low Glycaemic Index (GI) Diets

The glycaemic index (GI) rates carbohydrate rich foods on their effect on blood glucose levels. The GI has shown that not all starchy foods are digested and absorbed slowly and that some sugars and sugary foods are not digested and absorbed quickly as previously thought. Foods that have a low GI, cause a smaller and more gradual rise in blood glucose levels. High GI foods cause blood glucose levels to rise more quickly and to a higher level. The type of starch and sugar in the food, the acidity, fat, fibre content and degree of processing all affect the GI of a food. GI values should not be used in isolation but consideration should also be given to the energy, fat, sugar, fibre and salt content of the diet.

Some foods that have a low GI may also be high in fat and/or sugar and low in fibre. An example of this is chocolate and crisps. Low GI foods that are low in saturated fat and sugar and are high in fibre are recommended. A simple way to apply the GI is to include at least one low GI food, that is also high in fibre, at each meal or to use recipes that incorporate some low GI ingredients. NOSH recipes incorporate low GI foods where possible. Table 8 shows the GI of some commonly eaten foods.

For information on more foods, search the GI database on the following website: www.glycemicindex.com

Table 8: Glycaemic Index of Carbohydrate Rich Foods that are low in fat

	Low Glycaemic Index	Moderate Glycaemic Index	High Glycaemic Index
Breakfast Cereals and Grains	Allbran®, oat porridge, natural muesli, Special K®, Guardian®, bulghur wheat, oatbran	Weet–Bix®, Vita–Brits™, Just Right®, Fruitful Lite™, Nutrigrain®, couscous, cornmeal	Sultana Bran, Litebix™, Puffed Wheat, Instant Porridge™, Cornflakes, Ricebubbles®
Pasta and Rice	Wholemeal and white pasta Koshikari rice	Udon and dried rice noodles, Basmati and Doongara rice	Rice and corn pastas Brown and Jasmine rice
Breads	Breads with a high content of wholegrains and seeds, fruit bread	Light rye, Pita bread	Wheatmeal and grain breads with a high white flour content, white bread, bagels
Fruit	Apples, pears, oranges, berry and stone fruits, kiwi, yellow bananas, grapes, prunes, dried apricots	Apricots, cherries, pineapple, melon, spotty/brown bananas, figs, sultanas, raisins	Dates
Vegetables	Corn, yams, peas, legumes #	Beetroot, taro	Most potatoes, red kumara, parsnip, pumpkin, swede

\# Includes vegetables low in carbohydrate: asparagus, bok choy, broccoli, sprouts, cabbage, peppers, carrots, cauliflower, celery, leeks, lettuce, mushrooms, onions, silverbeet/spinach, tomatoes, zucchini.

soups

Soups are a great way of incorporating vegetables into the diet and including ones that you or your family, are not fond of individually. Soups can look boring – make them appealing by serving them in a nice bowl with a garnish and some fresh crusty bread on the side.

Soups make a great lunch meal, or a complete meal for dinner, if they are substantial. Leftover soup can be easily frozen – make sure it is cooled quickly before freezing. Thaw in the microwave, or overnight in the refrigerator and reheat until it is boiling.

NOSH has a range of soup recipes – some thick, some thin and some chunky. Even the creamy soups are low in fat compared to normal creamy soups.

Italian Vegetable Soup

This is a delicious chunky vegetable soup. The chilli beans add a little heat to the soup and lots of goodness. They are high in fibre and protein and have a low glycaemic index.

2 – 3 serves	4 – 6 serves	ingredients
½ medium	1 medium	red onion
¼ cup	½ cup	chopped lean bacon (optional)
½ teaspoon	1 teaspoon	vegetable oil
½ teaspoon	1 teaspoon	crushed garlic
4 cups (1 litre)	8 cups (2 litres)	cold water
1 teaspoon	2 teaspoons	beef or vegetable stock powder
1½ tablespoons	3 tablespoons	no added salt tomato paste
¼ teaspoon	½ teaspoon	ground pepper
½ teaspoon	1 teaspoon	dried mixed herbs
2 tablespoons	¼ cup	dry red wine
300 grams	600 grams	vegetables such as carrots, celery, kumara, parsnip, pumpkin
½ x 400 gram can	1 x 400 gram can	chilli beans
¼ cup	½ cup	uncooked penne pasta
Garnish sprinkle	sprinkle	parmesan flakes

1   Chop the onion and bacon into small cubes. Heat the oil in a large pan. Add the onion, bacon and garlic and fry over a medium heat until browned.
2   Add the water, stock, tomato paste, pepper, mixed herbs and wine. Simmer over a low heat.
3   Leaving the skins on, chop the vegetables into 1 cm cubes and add to the pan.
4   Bring to the boil then simmer for 1 hour. Stir occasionally.
5   Add the chilli beans and pasta. Cook, over a medium heat for a further 15 minutes.
6   To garnish, sprinkle over the parmesan.

Nutrition Information (per serve) based on serving 3 or 6
Energy: 717 kj (172 cal)   Carbohydrate: 28 g   Fibre: 7.0 g   Total fat: 2.2 g   Saturated fat: 0.6 g   Sodium: 689 mg   GI: Low
GF* Use GF stock powder, tomato paste, chilli beans and pasta.

Beef Goulash

This soup is like a tasty unthickened stew. Serve it with some wholegrain bread and it will make a great winter meal.

2 – 3 serves	4 – 6 serves	ingredients
½ medium	1 medium	onion
150 grams	300 grams	lean blade steak
½ teaspoon	1 teaspoon	olive oil
½ teaspoon	1 teaspoon	crushed garlic
½ x 400 gram can	1 x 400 gram can	tomatoes, in tomato juice
2 tablespoons	4 tablespoons	no added salt tomato paste
1 tablespoon	2 tablespoons	Worcestershire sauce
½ – 1 teaspoon	1 – 2 teaspoons	dried herbs such as basil, thyme, oregano
1 teaspoon	2 teaspoons	Vegemite™
3 cups (750 ml)	6 cups (1.5 litres)	cold water
½ small	1 small	zucchini
125 grams	250 grams	vegetables such as carrots, beans, pumpkin, celery
¼ cup	½ cup	chopped mushrooms (optional)
¼ cup	½ cup	dried pearl barley or brown lentils
to taste	to taste	ground pepper
Garnish sprinkle	sprinkle	fresh herbs

1. Chop the onion and meat into cubes. Heat the oil in a large pan with the garlic. Add the onion and meat and fry over a medium heat until browned.
2. Add the tomatoes, paste, sauce, herbs, vegemite and water. Simmer over a low heat.
3. Leaving the skins on, chop the zucchini and other vegetables into 1 cm cubes. Add to the pan along with the mushrooms and barley or lentils.
4. Bring to the boil then simmer for 1 hour uncovered or until the meat is tender and the barley or lentils are cooked. Stir occasionally. Season with pepper.
5. To garnish, sprinkle over the remaining herbs.

Nutrition Information (per serve) based on serving 3 or 6

Energy: 726 kj (174 cal)   Carbohydrate: 17 g   Fibre: 3.6 g   Total fat: 3.8 g   Saturated fat: 1.1 g   Sodium: 306 mg   GI: Low
GF* Use GF canned tomatoes, tomato paste, Worcestershire sauce and dried herbs. Replace Vegemite™ with a GF beef stock powder and use lentils in place of the barley.

Traditional Leek & Potato Soup

Most creamy soups are not low in fat. The cream style corn makes this soup creamy without the need to add butter or cream.

4 serves	ingredients
1 large	leek
2 small	potatoes
1 medium	orange kumara
1½ medium	carrots
2 rashers	lean bacon
2 teaspoons	chicken stock powder
1½ teaspoons	crushed garlic
¼ medium	leek
2 cups	low fat milk
1 x 400 gram can	cream style corn
1 teaspoon	French onion soup powder
to taste	ground pepper

1. Slice the first measure of leeks finely. Chop the potatoes, kumara, carrots and bacon into 1 cm cubes.
2. In a large pan combine the chopped vegetables and bacon with the stock and garlic. Just cover with water, bring to the boil and simmer for 15 – 20 minutes or until the vegetables are soft. Stir occasionally.
3. Meanwhile make the leek slivers by slicing the second measure of leeks into long thin strips. Place in a non–stick pan and lightly spray with oil. Cook over a low heat until browned and crisp. Stir often.
4. Add the milk, corn and soup powder to the soup mixture. Stir constantly over a low heat until hot. Do not boil as the soup may curdle.
5. Season with the pepper. To garnish, sprinkle over the fried leeks.

Nutrition Information (per serve)

Energy: 973 kj (232 cal) Carbohydrate: 42 g Fibre: 9.7 g Total fat: 2.4 g Saturated fat: 0.7 g
Sodium: 865 mg GI: Low GF* Use GF stock powder, cream style corn and French onion soup powder.

Bruschetta

Choose breads that are mainly grainy with a wholemeal base to them. Grainy breads have a lower glycaemic index (GI) than 100% wholemeal or white breads. Low GI foods are beneficial for weight loss and controlling blood glucose levels.

4 serves	ingredients
2	wholegrain bread rolls
½ cup	low fat cottage cheese
sprinkle	grated parmesan cheese
2 tablespoons	freshly chopped herbs
or 1 – 2 teaspoons	crushed garlic
or 4 teaspoons	pesto

1. Preheat the oven to 180°C (160°C fan).
2. Slice the rolls in half diagonally. Place on an oven tray.
3. Combine the cottage cheese with the parmesan cheese and either the herbs, garlic or pesto. Spread over the rolls.
4. Bake for 10 – 15 minutes until brown and crisp.

Nutrition Information (per serving) based on garlic flavour

Energy: 410 kj (98 cal) Carbohydrate: 14 g Fibre: 1.3 g Total fat: 1.1 g Saturated fat: 0.3 g
Sodium: 164 mg GI: Medium

Creamy Coconut & Red Curry Pumpkin Soup

Coconut is high in saturated fat, and therefore it should only be used in small amounts. Coconut flavoured evaporated milk is a great low fat substitute for coconut cream or milk.

	2 serves	4 serves	ingredients
	300 grams	600 grams	pumpkin
	¾ cup	1 ½ cups	cold water
	1 teaspoon	2 teaspoons	chicken or vegetable stock powder
	½ medium	1 medium	onion
	½ teaspoon	1 teaspoon	(70% fat) polyunsaturated margarine
	½ – 1 teaspoon	1 – 2 teaspoons	red curry paste
or	¼ – ½ teaspoon	½ – 1 teaspoon	curry powder
	½ teaspoon	1 teaspoon	crushed ginger
	½ cup	1 cup	creamy coconut flavoured light evaporated milk
	⅓ – ½ cup	⅔ – 1 cup	low fat milk
	to taste	to taste	ground pepper
Garnish	2 sprigs	4 sprigs	fresh coriander
	thin slivers	thin slivers	red and green pepper and red onion
	drizzle	drizzle	basil or sun dried tomato pesto

1. Scrub the pumpkin and cut into medium pieces. Place in a pan with the water and stock. Cook until it is soft. Remove the pumpkin from the pan and chop the skin off. Return to the pan.
2. Chop the onion into small cubes. Melt the margarine in a frying pan and add the onion, curry and ginger. Cook until the onion is soft. Add to the pumpkin mixture and leave to cool.
3. Purée with a food processor or a blender until smooth.
4. Place in a pan and add the coconut evaporated milk and then the low fat milk until the soup is of a desired consistency. Stir constantly over a low heat until hot. Season with the ground pepper.
5. To garnish, place the red and green peppers and onion slivers in the middle of each bowl in a crisscross pattern and top with the coriander. Drizzle the pesto around the garnish to form a circle.

Nutrition Information (per serve)

Energy: 704 kj (169 cal) Carbohydrate: 22 g Fibre: 5.1 g Fat: 2.8 g Saturated fat: 1.2 g Sodium: 526 mg GI: Low
GF* Use GF stock and coconut evaporated milk, curry powder or paste and pesto.

Creamy Coconut & Red Curry Pumpkin Soup (front) Tomato & Chargrilled Capsicum Soup pg 26 (middle)
and Traditional Leek & Potato Soup pg 23 (back)

Tomato & Chargrilled Capsicum Soup

This soup makes a refreshing change from the traditional tomato soup. The green and white ingredients provide a great contrast to the red – and they add texture.

	2 serves	4 serves	ingredients
	¼ medium	½ medium	green pepper
	¼ medium	½ medium	red pepper
	light spray	light spray	vegetable oil
	½ medium	1 medium	zucchini
	¼ medium	½ medium	red onion
	1 clove	2 cloves	garlic
	½ teaspoon	1 teaspoon	olive oil
	½ x 400 gram can	1 x 400 gram can	chopped tomatoes, in tomato juice
	½ cup	1 cup	canned chickpeas
	2¼ cups	4½ cups	tomato juice
	½ tablespoon	1 tablespoon	basil pesto
or	½ teaspoon	1 teaspoon	dried basil
	to taste	to taste	ground pepper
Garnish	2 sprigs	4 sprigs	fresh Italian parsley
	thin slivers	thin slivers	red and green pepper and red onion
	drizzle	drizzle	basil pesto

1. Remove the seeds from the first measure of red and green peppers and spray the skin side with oil. Place on a tray with the skin side up and grill until the skin turns black. Leave to cool, then remove the skin and chop the peppers into small pieces.
2. Chop the zucchini and onion into small cubes. Crush the garlic.
3. Heat the oil in a large pan. Add the onion and garlic and fry over a medium heat until browned.
4. Add the grilled peppers, zucchini, tomatoes, drained chickpeas, tomato juice and basil to the pan and stir.
5. Bring to the boil and then simmer for 30 minutes. Stir occasionally. Season with ground pepper.
6. To garnish, place the second measure of red and green peppers and onion slivers in the middle of each bowl in a crisscross pattern and top with the parsley. Drizzle the pesto around the garnish to form a circle.

Nutrition Information (per serve)

Energy: 709 kj (170 cal) Carbohydrate: 23 g Fibre: 5.2 g Fat: 5.5 g Saturated fat: 1.1 g Sodium: 549 mg GI: Low
GF* Use GF canned tomatoes, tomato juice and pesto.

Pea & Smoky Ham Soup

This soup is best left for a day before eating so that the flavours can develop. Stocks are often high in salt so there is no need to add additional salt to this soup. The smoked paprika is a way of getting a delicious smoked flavour without any fat.

4 – 6 serves	ingredients
1 cup	dried green split peas
1 medium	onion
100 grams	smoked lean ham
1 – 2 teaspoons	smoked paprika powder
3 cups (750 ml)	cold water
3 cups (750 ml)	liquid beef stock
2 small	potatoes
1 medium	carrot
1 large	leek
½ cup	frozen green peas
4 – 6 sprigs	fresh Italian parsley
thin slivers	red and green pepper
thin slivers	red onion
drizzle	sun dried tomato pesto

1 Place the split peas in a bowl and cover with cold water. Leave to soak for 2 hours then drain. Chop the onion and ham finely. Place in a large pan along with the split peas, paprika, water and stock.

2 Leaving the skins on, chop the potatoes and carrot into cubes. Wash the leek and slice finely. Add these vegetables to the pan. Bring to the boil then simmer for 1½ hours. Stir occasionally. Add the frozen peas. Cook for a further 5 minutes. Remove from the heat and leave to cool.

3 Purée with a food processor or a blender until smooth. Place in a bowl and cover. Refrigerate overnight for the flavours to develop.

4 Place in a pan. Bring to the boil then simmer for 15 minutes. Stir often.

5 To garnish, place the red and green peppers and onion slivers in the middle of each bowl in a crisscross pattern and top with the parsley. Drizzle the pesto around the garnish to form a circle.

Nutrition Information (per serve) based on serving 6

Energy: 754 kj (180 cal) Carbohydrate: 27 g Fibre: 4.9 g Total fat: 1.6 g Saturated fat: 0.6 g Sodium: 788 mg GI: Low GF* Use GF smoked paprika, beef stock and pesto.

Healthy Garlic Bread

Most garlic breads are laden with fat. This recipe uses only a small amount of a reduced fat margarine to carry the garlic flavour. Margarine is used in preference to butter as it contains far less saturated fats and is therefore more heart friendly.

4 serves	ingredients
4	wholegrain bread rolls
4 teaspoons	reduced fat (<56% fat) polyunsaturated margarine
1 – 2 teaspoons	crushed garlic

1 Preheat the oven to 180°C (160°C fan).

2 Make slices in the rolls at 3 cm intervals making sure not to chop right through the rolls.

3 Mix the margarine with the garlic. Spread lightly between the cuts.

4 Wrap in foil and bake for 15 minutes.

Nutrition Information (per serve)

Energy: 705 kj (169 cal) Carbohydrate: 28 g Fibre: 2.5 g Total fat: 3.8 g Saturated fat: 0.5 g Sodium: 284 mg GI: Medium

Thai Chicken & Rice Noodle Soup

This soup can be a one pot meal with its meat and vegetable combination. Try substituting the chicken with prawns or chunks of uncooked fish such as salmon or a white fleshed fish. Add the fish near the end of cooking to prevent it falling apart.

	2 serves	4 serves	ingredients
	200 grams	400 grams	fresh skinless and boneless chicken thighs
	1 medium	2 medium	red onion/s
	1 cup	2 cups	chopped yams or carrots
	½ medium	1 medium	red pepper
	1 teaspoon	2 teaspoons	crushed garlic
	1 teaspoon	2 teaspoons	crushed ginger
	2 teaspoons	4 teaspoons	red curry paste
	1½ cups	3 cups	liquid chicken stock
	½ cup	1 cup	creamy coconut flavoured light evaporated milk
	50 grams	100 grams	dried rice noodles
	¾ cup	1½ cups	broccoli florets or chopped bok choy
	½ cup	1 cup	frozen whole green beans
Garnish	10	20	cashews
	6 – 9	12 – 18	sprouted pea shoots

1. Chop the chicken into small cubes.
2. Chop the onion/s into wedges and the yams or carrots into 2 cm cubes. Slice the red pepper into strips. In a large pan cook the onion with the garlic, ginger and curry paste for 1 minute.
3. Add the chicken and cook for 2 minutes. Add the yams or carrots, red pepper, stock and coconut evaporated milk. Simmer until the vegetables are tender.
4. Cook the noodles according to the instructions on the packet. Drain.
5. Add the noodles, broccoli or bok choy and beans to the soup. Cook over a low heat until the vegetables are tender. Stir frequently to stop the soup sticking to the bottom of the pan.
6. To garnish, sprinkle with cashews and pea shoots if desired.

Nutrition Information (per serve)

Energy: 1116 kj (268 cal)   Carbohydrate: 31 g   Fibre: 3.9 g   Total fat: 4.3 g   Saturated fat: 1.3 g   Sodium: 745 mg   GI: Low

GF* Use GF curry paste, chicken stock and coconut evaporated milk.

salads & vegetables

Mediterranean Style Tomatoes pg 44

Artichoke

Italian Potato Bake pg 40

Are you bored with vegetables and you just eat them because you know that they are good for you? Well, make your vegetables interesting – how many foods do we eat without adding some form of flavour? NOSH recipes add flavour without adding lots of fat and salt. There is also an emphasis on presenting them nicely – this does help make your food look more appetising.

Vegetables cannot be replaced with supplements – supplements may contain the vitamins and minerals, found in vegetables, but they won't contain all of the anti–cancer substances found or any of those yet to be discovered. Vegetables also contain fibre, which is not often included in supplements. Aim to eat at least 3 – 4 servings, of different coloured vegetables, a day. Where possible leave the skins on and eat some raw as snacks or as part of a salad.

Green Bean & Chickpea Salad

I assure you that this is not a boring bean salad! It's colourful, tasty and nutritious. It is important to eat a variety of coloured vegetables – this will decrease your risk of heart disease and some diet related cancers.

2 serves	4 serves	ingredients
5	10	fresh green beans
¼ small	½ small	red onion
⅓ cup	⅔ cup	canned kidney beans
⅓ cup	⅔ cup	canned chickpeas
2 tablespoons	¼ cup	chopped red pepper
2 tablespoons	¼ cup	chopped celery
¼ cup	½ cup	pineapple juice
1 tablespoon	2 tablespoons	balsamic vinegar
1½ teaspoons	1 tablespoon	olive oil
½ teaspoon	1 teaspoon	crushed garlic
½ teaspoon	1 teaspoon	lightly packed brown sugar
⅛ teaspoon	¼ teaspoon	ground pepper
¼ cup	½ cup	canned pineapple pieces, in natural juice
⅛ – ¼ cup	¼ – ½ cup	fresh herbs such as Italian parsley or coriander

1. Chop the green beans into 4 cm lengths. Steam until just tender and then rinse in cold water to stop them cooking. Drain.
2. Finely slice the onion.
3. Place the kidney beans and chickpeas in a sieve and rinse under running water. Drain.
4. Combine the green beans, onion, kidney beans, chickpeas, red pepper and celery in a bowl.
5. Combine the pineapple juice, vinegar, oil, garlic, sugar and ground pepper in a saucepan. Bring to the boil then remove from the heat. Cool, then pour over the vegetable mixture.
6. Place in the refrigerator. Leave for 24 hours for the flavours to be absorbed into the vegetables.
7. Just before serving slice the pineapple and herbs into small pieces and stir through.

Nutrition Information (per serve)

Energy: 576 kj (138 cal) Carbohydrate: 18 g Fibre: 4.4 g Total fat: 5.1 g Saturated fat: 1.1 g Sodium: 155 mg GI: Low
GF* No modifications needed.

Classic Coleslaw

The dressing in this recipe is low in fat compared to many creamy dressings, and the mint is a refreshing addition. A low fat, bought dressing, can replace the yoghurt and sour cream.

2 serves	4 serves	ingredients
1 ½ cups	3 cups	finely sliced cabbage
¼ medium	½ medium	red skinned eating apple
¼ medium	½ medium	orange
1 small	2 small	spring onion/s
1 tablespoon	2 tablespoons	sultanas
1 tablespoon	2 tablespoons	low fat plain yoghurt
1 teaspoon	2 teaspoons	reduced fat sour cream
½ teaspoon	1 teaspoon	whole seed mustard
½ – 1 tablespoon	1 – 2 tablespoons	chopped fresh mint
1 tablespoon	2 tablespoons	toasted pumpkin kernels

1 Finely slice the cabbage. Leaving the skin on the apple, core and chop into cubes. Chop the orange into cubes, the onion into chunks and the sultanas in half.
2 Combine the yoghurt, sour cream, mustard and mint.
3 Combine all the ingredients and mix well. Refrigerate for 15 minutes to allow the mint flavour to develop.

Nutrition Information (per serve)
Energy: 410 kj (98 cal)   Carbohydrate: 11 g   Fibre: 2 g
Total fat: 4 g   Saturated fat: 0.9 g   Sodium: 58 mg
GI: Low   GF* Use GF yoghurt, sour cream and whole seed mustard.

Fruity Waldorf Salad

This is a refreshing salad and a great way to eat more fruit. Try to eat at least 3 – 4 pieces, a day, of different coloured varieties. Leave the skin on where practical as this contains fibre.

2 serves	4 serves	ingredients
½ medium	1 medium	orange
8	16	black grapes
1	2	red skinned eating apple/s
¼ cup	½ cup	chopped celery
2 tablespoons	¼ cup	chopped walnuts
2 tablespoons	¼ cup	low fat plain yoghurt
½ teaspoon	1 teaspoon	lemon juice
½ teaspoon	1 teaspoon	grated lemon rind
1 teaspoon	2 teaspoons	poppy seeds

1 Chop the orange into cubes and the grapes in half.
2 Leaving the skin on the apple/s, core and chop into cubes.
3 Combine the fruit, celery and walnuts together.
4 Combine the yoghurt, lemon juice, rind and seeds.
5 Mix through the salad.
6 Serve within 30 minutes of being prepared.

Nutrition Information (per serve)
Energy: 501 kj (120 cal)   Carbohydrate: 14 g   Fibre: 2 g
Total fat: 5.7 g   Saturated fat: 0.7 g   Sodium: 29 mg
GI: Low   GF* Use GF yoghurt.

Mixed Leaf Salad

I was never a green salad fan until I discovered balsamic vinaigrette – it adds a lot of flavour to a salad. The fancy leaf lettuces and the salad herbs that are now readily available have modernised lettuce salad.

	2 serves	4 serves	ingredients
	1½ cups	3 cups	salad herbs or mixed leaf lettuce
	2 tablespoons	4 tablespoons	cucumber
	4	8	cherry tomatoes
	2 tablespoons	4 tablespoons	sun dried tomatoes or red pepper
	2 tablespoons	4 tablespoons	spring onion or avocado
or	6	12	whole blanched beans
	4	8	black olives or grapes
	1 tablespoon	2 tablespoons	diced feta cheese
or	sprinkle	sprinkle	parmesan flakes
	2 teaspoons	4 teaspoons	pine nuts or cashews

1. Wash the vegetables and fruit. Place half of the salad leaves in a salad bowl.
2. Chop the vegetables into smaller pieces. Cut the olives or grapes in half.
3. Scatter half of the vegetables, fruit, cheese and nuts over the leaves.
4. Place the remaining leaves over the top then scatter over the remaining ingredients.
5. Serve with a vinaigrette (page 38).

Nutrition Information (per serve)

Energy: 367 kj (88 cal) Carbohydrate: 3 g Fibre: 2.3 g Total fat: 7.2 g Saturated fat: 1.9 g Sodium: 114 mg GI: Low
GF* No modifications needed.

Hot Smoked Salmon Nicoise Salad

The smoked salmon is a delicious variation to this salad which is traditionally made with tuna. The sun dried tomato pesto vinaigrette just finishes it off.

2 serves	4 serves	ingredients
1½ medium	3 medium	new potatoes
1 medium	2 medium	egg/s
6	12	whole green beans
2 cups	4 cups	curly lettuce
1 medium	2 medium	tomato/es
50 grams	100 grams	feta cheese
100 grams	200 grams	hot smoked salmon
4	8	black olives
1 teaspoon	2 teaspoons	pine nuts
¼ cup	½ cup	balsamic vinegar
1 teaspoon	2 teaspoons	sun dried tomato pesto

1. Scrub the potatoes and chop into 3 cm cubes. Cook until just tender and leave to cool.
2. Boil the egg/s for 7 minutes. Cool, remove the shells and chop into 4 wedges.
3. Steam the beans until just tender. Cool.
4. Tear the lettuce into palm–size pieces. Chop each tomato into wedges, the feta cheese into cubes, the salmon into chunks and the olives in half.
5. In a bowl place the lettuce and salmon, then scatter over the vegetables, egg, cheese and nuts.
6. Shake the vinegar and pesto together. Pour over the salad and serve immediately.

Nutrition Information (per serve)

Energy: 1254 kj (300 cal) Carbohydrate: 22 g Fibre: 4.8 g Total fat: 13.4 g Saturated fat: 5.1 g Sodium: 1405 mg GI: Medium
GF* Use GF pesto.

Roast Vegetable Salad (back) and Mixed Leaf Salad pg 33 (front)

Roast Vegetable Salad

To increase the fibre of your diet, leave the skins on vegetables where possible. Replace salt in recipes with herbs and spices.

2 serves	4 serves	ingredients
2 cups	4 cups	mixed chopped vegetables such as potatoes, orange kumara, pumpkin, parsnip, yams and carrots
½ medium	1 medium	red onion
¼ medium	½ medium	red pepper
1 small	2 small	zucchini
light spray	light spray	olive oil
2 large cloves	4 large cloves	garlic
1 – 1½ teaspoons	2 – 3 teaspoons	dried herbs such as rosemary, basil, smoked paprika powder
sprinkle	sprinkle	ground pepper
2 tablespoons	¼ cup	balsamic vinegar
1 teaspoon	2 teaspoons	olive oil

1. Preheat the oven to 200°C (180°C fan).
2. Scrub the mixed vegetables. Chop all the vegetables into 3 cm cubes. Place in a pan, except the onion, red pepper and zucchini. Cover with water and boil for 5 minutes. Drain.
3. Place on a tray, lined with baking paper. Lightly spray with oil.
4. Chop each garlic clove into 4 pieces. Sprinkle the garlic, herbs, ground pepper and half of the vinegar over the vegetables. Bake for 10 minutes. Stir and then cook for another 10 minutes.
5. Add the onion, red pepper and the zucchini and stir gently through. Lightly spray with oil. Cook for a further 15 – 20 minutes or until the vegetables are cooked and brown.
6. Shake the remaining vinegar and oil together until combined. Pour over the vegetables and mix together gently.
7. Best served warm.

Nutrition Information (per serve)
Energy: 674 kj (161 cal) Carbohydrate: 28 g Fibre: 4.9 g Total fat: 4.1 g Saturated fat: 0.7 g Sodium: 24 mg GI: Medium
GF* Use GF herbs and paprika.

Yoghurt Style Dressing

This is a quick and easy creamy dressing to make. Add your own choice of seasoning.

½ cup	1 cup	ingredients
⅓ cup	⅔ cup	low fat plain yoghurt
¼ teaspoon	½ teaspoon	balsamic vinegar
as required	as required	low fat milk
		seasoning:
to taste	to taste	pepper
or 1 tablespoon	2 tablespoons	chopped fresh herbs
or 1 teaspoon	2 teaspoons	whole seed mustard
or 1 teaspoon	2 teaspoons	pesto

1. Mix the yoghurt and vinegar together.
2. Add the seasoning of your choice.
3. Add some low fat milk until a desired consistency is achieved.
4. Place in a sealed container and refrigerate. The dressing will last for up to 2 days.

Nutrition Information (per teaspoon) unseasoned
Energy: 11 kj (2.6 cal) Carbohydrate: 0.4 g Fibre: 0.01 g
Total fat: 0.03 g Saturated fat: 0 g Sodium: 2 mg
GI: Low   GF* Use GF yoghurt, whole seed mustard and pesto.

Balsamic Vinaigrette

Most vinaigrettes contain equal quantities of oil and vinegar which make them high in kilojoules. This recipe uses only a small amount of olive oil – the better quality the oil is, the nicer the vinaigrette will taste.

½ cup	1 cup	ingredients
⅓ cup	⅔ cup	balsamic vinegar
1 tablespoon	2 tablespoons	olive oil
		seasoning:
1 tablespoon	2 tablespoons	chopped fresh herbs
or 1 teaspoon	2 teaspoons	whole seed mustard
or 1 teaspoon	2 teaspoons	pesto

1. Combine the vinegar and oil with your choice of seasoning and mix well.
2. Place in a sealed container and refrigerate. The vinaigrette will last for up to 2 weeks.
3. Shake before using.

Nutrition Information (per teaspoon) unseasoned
Energy: 22 kj (5 cal) Carbohydrate: 0.03 g Fibre: 0 g
Total fat: 0.6 g Saturated fat: 0.09 g Sodium: 0.8 mg
GI: Low   GF* Use GF whole seed mustard and pesto.

Asian Style Rice Salad

This salad uses brown rice which gives it a nutty flavour. Brown rice contains more fibre than white rice as it hasn't had all of its outer shells removed.

2 – 3 serves	4 – 6 serves	ingredients
2 cups	4 cups	cold water
½ cup	1 cup	uncooked brown rice
½ teaspoon	1 teaspoon	iodised salt
¼ cup	½ cup	canned pineapple pieces, in natural juice
¼ cup	½ cup	pineapple juice
¾ teaspoon	1½ teaspoons	olive oil
2 teaspoons	4 teaspoons	Worcestershire sauce
¼ teaspoon	½ teaspoon	crushed garlic
½ teaspoon	1 teaspoon	crushed ginger
¼ cup	½ cup	canned chickpeas
1½ tablespoons	3 tablespoons	diced spring onion
1½ tablespoons	3 tablespoons	diced red pepper
1½ tablespoons	3 tablespoons	raisins
2½ tablespoons	5 tablespoons	dry roasted cashews or peanuts
1 tablespoon	2 tablespoons	sesame seeds
1 teaspoon	2 teaspoons	poppy seeds

1. Place the cold water, rice and salt in a pan. Bring to the boil and simmer for 25 – 35 minutes or until just cooked. The rice should be still slightly firm to bite.
2. While the rice is cooking, drain the juice from the pineapple. Measure the required quantity of the juice and combine with the oil, Worcestershire sauce, garlic and ginger.
3. When the rice is cooked, drain the excess water from the pan. Stir the pineapple juice mixture and drained chickpeas gently through the hot rice. Simmer over a low heat for 5 minutes. Cool and then refrigerate for at least 2 hours.
4. Chop each piece of pineapple into 3 strips. Stir gently through the rice along with the spring onion, red pepper, raisins, nuts and seeds. Refrigerate until serving.

Nutrition Information (per serve) based on serving 3 or 6

Energy: 1005 kj (240 cal) Carbohydrate: 36 g Fibre: 2.7 g Total fat: 8.4 g Saturated fat: 1.5 g Sodium: 507 mg GI: Medium
GF* Use GF Worcestershire sauce.

Italian Potato Bakes

The evaporated milk in this dish makes a great substitute for cream with only 6% fat compared with 40%. The key is to thicken the milk to give a smoother texture and to stop it curdling.

2 serves	4 serves	ingredients
2 medium	4 medium	potatoes
½ medium	1 medium	red onion
½ medium	1 medium	red pepper
1 cup	2 cups	torn and lightly packed spinach
⅔ cup	1⅓ cups	reduced fat evaporated milk
2 teaspoons	4 teaspoons	sun dried tomato pesto
1 teaspoon	2 teaspoons	crushed garlic
½ teaspoon	1 teaspoon	chicken or vegetable stock powder
1 teaspoon	2 teaspoons	no added salt tomato paste
2 teaspoons	4 teaspoons	reduced fat evaporated milk
1 teaspoon	2 teaspoons	cornflour
1 tablespoon	2 tablespoons	grated parmesan cheese

1 | Preheat the oven to 180°C (160°C).
2 | Scrub the potatoes then slice into thin rounds. Place in a pan, cover with water and bring to the boil. Drain.
3 | Chop the onion into rings and the red pepper into strips. Wash the spinach and drain well.
4 | Place one third of the potatoes in the bottom of 2 – 4 (¾ cup) individual ramekins. Scatter over half of the spinach, onion and red pepper. Place another layer of potatoes on top then scatter over the remaining spinach, onion and red pepper. Place a final layer of potato on top.
5 | Combine the first measure of evaporated milk with the pesto, garlic, stock and paste in a pan.
6 | Bring to the boil. Mix the second measure of evaporated milk and cornflour to a paste. Add to the pan and stir until it starts to thicken. Remove from the heat.
7 | Pour the milk mixture over the layered vegetables. Sprinkle over the parmesan.
8 | Bake for 30 – 40 minutes or until the potatoes are cooked. If the bakes are browning too much, place some aluminium foil over the top during cooking.

Nutrition Information (per serve)

Energy: 1045 kj (250 cal) Carbohydrate: 38 g Fibre: 3.4 g Total fat: 5.2 g Saturated fat: 1.9 g Sodium: 310 mg GI: Medium
GF* Use GF evaporated milk, pesto, stock, paste and cornflour.

Corn & Cheese Topped Potatoes

These potatoes have less fat than a baked potato served with butter or sour cream – and much more flavour.

	2 serves	4 serves	ingredients
	2 medium	4 medium	potatoes
	light spray	light spray	oil
	1	2	spring onion/s
or	½ small	1 small	red onion
	¼ medium	½ medium	red pepper
	1 rasher	2 rashers	lean bacon
or	1 slice	2 slices	ham
	¼ cup	½ cup	canned cream style corn
	¼ cup	½ cup	low fat cottage cheese
	¼ teaspoon	½ teaspoon	French onion soup powder
	sprinkle	sprinkle	grated parmesan cheese
Garnish	4 sprigs	8 sprigs	fresh herbs

1. Preheat the oven to 200°C (180°C fan).
2. Scrub the potatoes. Spray with oil and bake for 50 – 60 minutes or until cooked.
3. Slice the onion, red pepper and bacon or ham finely. Cook in a non–stick frying pan until the onion and bacon/ham have browned.
4. Remove from the heat and add the corn, cottage cheese and soup powder. Mix well.
5. Slice the potatoes in half lengthwise. Spread over the topping and sprinkle with the parmesan cheese.
6. Bake for a further 10 – 15 minutes until browned. Serve with some sprigs of herbs.

Nutrition Information (per serve)

Energy: 799 kj (191 cal)   Carbohydrate: 30 g   Fibre: 4.3 g   Total fat: 2.4 g   Saturated fat: 1.1 g   Sodium: 323 mg   GI: High
GF* Use GF cream style corn, cottage cheese and soup powder.

Roasted Mediterranean Style Tomatoes

Most of us probably eat our tomatoes uncooked. Try cooking them for a change. These slowly roasted tomatoes are simple to make – don't overcook them as they will split.

2 serves	4 serves	ingredients
2 medium	4 medium	tomatoes
1 teaspoon	2 teaspoons	basil pesto
1 thin slice	2 thin slices	feta cheese
2	4	black olives

1. Preheat the oven to 150°C (130°C fan).
2. Slice the tomatoes in half. Place the sliced side up in an ovenproof dish.
3. Spread the pesto on top of the tomatoes.
4. Chop the feta cheese into small triangles. Place a triangle on top of each tomato.
5. Cut the olives in half. Place a halved olive on top of the feta cheese.
6. Bake for 20 – 30 minutes until cooked.

Nutrition Information (per serve)
Energy: 181 kj (43 cal) Carbohydrate: 4 g Fibre: 1.6 g
Total fat: 2.4 g Saturated fat: 0.6 g Sodium: 113 mg
GI: Low GF* Use GF pesto.

Grated Zucchini with Corn & Peppers

This is a tasty way of serving zucchini. Adding corn, to this dish, adds colour and a different texture. Corn is high in fibre and has a low glycaemic index.

2 serves	4 serves	ingredients
½ medium	1 medium	red onion
½ small	1 small	red pepper
1 medium	2 medium	zucchini
½ teaspoon	1 teaspoon	reduced fat (<56% fat) polyunsaturated margarine
½ teaspoon	1 teaspoon	crushed ginger
1 teaspoon	2 teaspoons	honey
½ cup	1 cup	frozen corn kernels
to taste	to taste	ground pepper

1. Chop the onion and red pepper into small cubes. Grate the zucchini.
2. Melt the margarine in a frying pan and add the onion, red pepper, zucchini, ginger, honey and corn. Cook until the onion and zucchini are cooked.
3. Season with ground pepper.

Nutrition Information (per serve)
Energy: 362 kj (87 cal) Carbohydrate: 15 g Fibre: 2.3 g
Total fat: 1.7 g Saturated fat: 0.3 g Sodium: 12 mg
GI: Low GF* No modifications needed.

Roasted Mediterranean Style Tomatoes

Beans with sautéed Bacon and Pinenuts

Beans with sautéed Bacon & Pinenuts

Steaming vegetables will prevent the loss of some vitamins and minerals. Aim to eat at least 3 – 4 servings of different coloured vegetables daily.

2 serves	4 serves	ingredients
¼ medium	½ medium	red onion
¼ medium	½ medium	red pepper
1½ cups	3 cups	fresh or frozen whole green beans
½ teaspoon	1 teaspoon	crushed garlic
2 tablespoons	¼ cup	diced lean bacon
1 teaspoon	2 teaspoons	pine nuts
sprinkle	sprinkle	black pepper

1. Chop the onion and red pepper into small cubes.
2. If using fresh beans remove the tops. Steam the beans until cooked. Keep warm.
3. In a non–stick frying pan fry the onion, pepper, garlic and bacon until cooked. Stir through the nuts.
4. Place the beans on a plate, sprinkle the mixture over and some ground pepper.

Nutrition Information (per serve)
Energy: 178 kj (43 cal) **Carbohydrate:** 5 g **Fibre:** 2.6 g
Total fat: 1.4 g **Saturated fat:** 0.3 g **Sodium:** 95 mg
GI: Low **GF*** No modifications needed.

Orange & Marmalade Glaze for Carrots or Yams

The marmalade, while it may seem unusual, is a great combination with the carrots or yams.

	2 serves	4 serves	ingredients
	2 – 3 medium	4 – 6 medium	carrots
or	6 medium	12 medium	yams
	1 tablespoon	2 tablespoons	concentrated apple and orange juice
	¼ cup	½ cup	cold water
	½ tablespoon	1 tablespoon	medium white wine
	¼ teaspoon	½ teaspoon	crushed ginger
	1 tablespoon	2 tablespoons	marmalade
	sprinkle	sprinkle	sesame seeds

1. Scrub the carrots and slice as desired. If using yams, scrub then trim the tops and bottoms.
2. Steam the carrots or yams until cooked but still firm. Keep warm.
3. Combine the juice, water, wine, ginger and marmalade in a pan.
4. Bring to the boil and cook until thick and syrupy.
5. Pour over the cooked carrots or yams.
6. Sprinkle with sesame seeds.

Nutrition Information (per serve)
Energy: 269 kj (64 cal) **Carbohydrate:** 13 g **Fibre:** 2.3 g
Total fat: 0.8 g **Saturated fat:** 0.1 g **Sodium:** 21 mg
GI: Low – Medium **GF*** No modifications needed.

pasta & rice

Green Bean Risotto pg 56

Fresh Fettuccine

Spaghetti Bolognese pg 53

Don't avoid high carbohydrate foods even though it may be fashionable to! Carbohydrates provide necessary fuel for the body and are no more fattening than most foods. They are often made fattening by the way they are prepared and served. Like anything – if you over indulge you will put on weight.

Try to replace potatoes with pasta and rice, at least twice a week. Pasta and some rice varieties, such as basmati and parboiled rice, have a lower glycaemic index (GI) than potatoes and brown rice. Potatoes and brown rice are still great foods – just include them as part of a meal with other low GI foods. If you haven't tried pasta, or you have tried it, and didn't like it – don't give up. You can learn to like pasta – the key is to serve it with tasty ingredients and not too much sauce. Eat the pasta with the sauce – if you eat the pasta by itself then it will be bland and boring. The same goes for rice.

Vegetarian Thai Chickpea & Kumara on Rice Noodles

Rice noodles are not as heavy as pasta and are even quicker to cook. Chickpeas add a nice, nutty flavour to this dish and they are high in fibre and protein and have a low glycaemic index.

	2 serves	4 serves	ingredients
	1 small	2 small	red onion/s
	½ medium	1 medium	orange kumara
	½ medium	1 medium	red pepper
	½ teaspoon	1 teaspoon	crushed ginger
	2 teaspoons	4 teaspoons	red curry paste
	½ x 375 gram can	1 x 375 gram can	creamy coconut flavoured light evaporated milk
	½ cup	1 cup	liquid vegetable stock
	100 grams	200 grams	uncooked rice noodles
	1 cup	2 cups	broccoli florets
	½ cup	1 cup	canned chickpeas
	½ cup	1 cup	low fat milk
	1 teaspoon	2 teaspoons	cornflour
Garnish	1 tablespoon	2 tablespoons	cashews
	1 tablespoon	2 tablespoons	chopped fresh coriander (optional)

1. Chop the onion/s into small wedges. Chop the kumara and red pepper into cubes.
2. In a non–stick frying pan fry the onion, kumara and red pepper with the ginger and curry paste for a couple of minutes. Add the evaporated milk and stock. Simmer until the kumara is tender.
3. While the vegetables are cooking, cook the noodles according to the instructions on the packet. When cooked, drain and keep warm.
4. Add the broccoli and drained chickpeas to the vegetable mixture. Cook until the broccoli is a bright green colour.
5. Add the low fat milk and heat until hot. Avoid boiling as the sauce may curdle. Mix the cornflour with a little water to form a smooth paste. Add and stir gently until thickened.
6. Serve over the noodles. Sprinkle over the nuts and coriander. Serve with a green leafy salad.

Nutrition Information (per serve) not including a salad side dish

Energy: 1585 kj (380 cal) Carbohydrate: 55 g Fibre: 6.4 g Total fat: 6.8 g Saturated fat: 2.4 g Sodium: 694 mg GI: Low
GF* Use GF curry paste, evaporated milk, stock and cornflour.

Pasta with a Roast Vegetable Medley

Pasta is a great alternative to potatoes as it has a lower glycaemic index. This vegetable medley is light and refreshing.

2 serves	4 serves	ingredients
3 medium	6 medium	tomatoes
½ medium	1 medium	red onion
1 medium	2 medium	zucchini
6	12	button mushrooms
¼ medium	½ medium	red pepper
6	12	black or green olives
4 cloves	8 cloves	garlic
1 teaspoon	2 teaspoons	coriander seeds
1	2	bay leaf/leaves
sprinkle	sprinkle	ground pepper
2 tablespoons	4 tablespoons	balsamic vinegar
2 cups (110 grams)	4 cups (220 grams)	uncooked penne pasta
2 tablespoons	4 tablespoons	no added salt tomato paste
¼ cup	½ cup	liquid vegetable stock
2 tablespoons	4 tablespoons	dry white wine
⅓ cup	⅔ cup	fresh or frozen green beans
Garnish sprinkle	sprinkle	pine nuts
sprinkle	sprinkle	grated parmesan cheese
2 tablespoons	4 tablespoons	chopped fresh basil or parsley

1. Preheat the oven to 180°C (160°C fan).
2. Chop the tomatoes and onion into wedges, zucchini into thin rounds, mushrooms and red pepper into chunks. Halve the olives, slice the garlic cloves into thin slivers and crush the coriander seeds.
3. Place the tomatoes, onion, mushrooms, red pepper, olives, garlic, coriander, bay leaf/leaves, ground pepper and vinegar into a covered ovenproof dish. Cook for 30 – 40 minutes or until cooked.
4. Cook the pasta according to the instructions on the packet. When cooked, drain and keep warm.
5. While the pasta is cooking, drain the liquid from the vegetables into a frying pan. Add the paste, stock, wine, beans and zucchini. Simmer until the sauce has thickened. Add the roasted vegetables and heat through.
6. Serve over the pasta and sprinkle with the pine nuts, cheese and herbs.

Nutrition Information (per serve)

Energy: 1342 kj (321 cal) Carbohydrate: 50 g Fibre: 9.7 g Total fat: 5.4 g Saturated fat: 1.3 g Sodium: 529 mg GI: Low
GF* Use GF pasta, tomato paste and stock.

Spaghetti Bolognese

The inclusion of legumes and vegetables extends the mince and adds colour to this dish. Using lean mince is preferable due to its lower saturated fat content.

2 serves	4 serves	ingredients
½ medium	1 medium	onion
1 medium	2 medium	carrot/s
½ medium	1 medium	red pepper
1 medium	2 medium	zucchini
200 grams	400 grams	lean mince such as topside
¼ cup	½ cup	canned kidney beans
1 cup	2 cups	tomato pasta sauce
1 tablespoon	2 tablespoons	Worcestershire sauce
¼ cup	½ cup	dry red wine
110 grams	220 grams	uncooked spaghetti
Garnish sprinkle	sprinkle	parmesan cheese

1   Dice the onion, carrot/s, red pepper and zucchini into small cubes. Place in a frying pan with the mince and fry until the mince browns.
2   Add the drained kidney beans, pasta sauce, Worcestershire sauce and wine. Simmer for 10 – 15 minutes until the sauce thickens and the vegetables are cooked.
3   Meanwhile cook the spaghetti according to the instructions on the packet. When cooked, drain and keep warm.
4   Serve the mince over the spaghetti. Sprinkle with the parmesan cheese and serve with a green leafy salad.

Nutrition Information (per serve) not including a salad side dish
Energy: 2082 kj (498 cal)   Carbohydrate: 59 g   Fibre: 6.2 g   Total fat: 9.1 g   Saturated fat: 3.4 g   Sodium: 797 mg   GI: Low
GF* Use GF tomato pasta and Worcestershire sauces and GF spaghetti.

Creamy Tomato & Chicken Fettuccine

This is a quick pasta dish which uses sour cream to make it creamy and slightly acidic. Dairy foods can be high in fat, particularly saturated fat, so where possible choose low or reduced fat varieties.

2 serves	4 serves	ingredients
½ medium	1 medium	red onion
½ medium	1 medium	red pepper
4	8	button mushrooms
200 grams	400 grams	skinless and boneless chicken breasts
125 grams	250 grams	uncooked fettuccine
1 teaspoon	2 teaspoons	vegetable oil
1 teaspoon	2 teaspoons	crushed garlic
1 teaspoon	2 teaspoons	crushed ginger
1½ cups	3 cups	tomato pasta sauce
1 cup	2 cups	broccoli florets
3 tablespoons	6 tablespoons	reduced fat sour cream

1. Chop the onion, red pepper and mushrooms into chunks. Slice the chicken into long thin strips.
2. Cook the pasta according to the instructions on the packet. When cooked, drain and keep warm.
3. While the pasta is cooking, place the oil in a frying pan. When hot add the onion, red pepper, chicken, garlic and ginger. Fry for 2 minutes.
4. Add the pasta sauce and cook until the sauce has thickened and the chicken is cooked. Add the broccoli and mushrooms and cook for another 2 minutes.
5. Remove from the heat and stir through the sour cream. Serve over the pasta. Serve with stir–fried vegetables or a salad.

Nutrition Information (per serve) not including vegetable or salad side dishes
Energy: 1813 kj (435 cal)   Carbohydrate: 53 g   Fibre: 6 g   Total fat: 8.6 g   Saturated fat: 2.2 g   Sodium: 207 mg   GI: Low
GF* Use GF pasta, tomato pasta sauce and sour cream.

Spinach, Bacon & Mushroom Fettuccine

Creamy pasta sauces are generally high in fat as they tend to use cream. The evaporated milk and cheese slices give this sauce a similar richness to cream with much less fat.

2 serves	4 serves	ingredients
½ medium	1 medium	red pepper
½ medium	1 medium	onion
4 medium	8 medium	mushrooms
2 rashers	4 rashers	lean bacon such as chicken bacon
4	8	sun dried tomatoes
110 grams	220 grams	uncooked fettuccine
1 teaspoon	2 teaspoons	crushed garlic
½ x 375 ml can	1 x 375 ml can	reduced fat evaporated milk
1 cup	2 cups	torn and lightly packed spinach
1	2	tasty flavoured processed cheese slice/s
1 teaspoon	2 teaspoons	cornflour
¼ cup	½ cup	low fat milk
sprinkle	sprinkle	ground pepper
sprinkle	sprinkle	grated parmesan

1 Place the red pepper, skin facing upwards, under the grill until the skin is blackened. Cool, then remove the skin and chop the red pepper into chunks.

2 Slice the onion and mushrooms thinly. Chop the bacon and sun dried tomatoes into long strips.

3 Cook the pasta according to the instructions on the packet. When cooked, drain and keep warm.

4 While the pasta is cooking, fry the onion, mushrooms, bacon and garlic in a non–stick frying pan until browned and cooked.

5 Reduce the heat and add the evaporated milk. When the milk is hot add the red pepper, sun dried tomatoes, spinach and cheese slice/s.

6 Mix the cornflour in the low fat milk to form a smooth paste. Add to the sauce and stir over a low heat until the sauce thickens slightly. Add the ground pepper.

7 Serve over the pasta and sprinkle with parmesan. Serve with a green leafy salad.

Nutrition Information (per serve) not including a salad side dish

Energy: 1754 kj (420 cal) Carbohydrate: 60 g Fibre: 4.9 g Total fat: 7.6 g Saturated fat: 3.7 g Sodium: 878 mg GI: Low
GF* Use GF pasta, evaporated milk, cheese slices and cornflour.

Green Bean Risotto with Yams or Kumara

Authentic risottos are made creamy by adding generous amounts of cheese and butter and through constant stirring. The cheese slices create a creaminess, with less fat, and eliminate the need for constant stirring.

2 serves	4 serves	ingredients
½ cup	1 cup	chopped yams or orange kumara
1 medium	2 medium	red onion/s
2 large cloves	4 large cloves	garlic
6	12	button mushrooms
¾ cup	1½ cups	fresh or frozen whole baby green beans
½ tablespoon	1 tablespoon	reduced fat (<56% fat) polyunsaturated margarine
¾ cup	1½ cups	Arborio or short grain rice
1½ cups	3 cups	liquid vegetable stock
¾ cup	1½ cups	dry white wine
½ cup	1 cup	cold water
1	2	tasty flavoured processed cheese slice/s
sprinkle	sprinkle	cracked pepper

1   Place the yams or kumara in a pan, cover with water and boil until just tender. Drain.
2   Chop the onion/s into small wedges. Finely slice the garlic.
3   Chop the mushrooms and fresh beans in half. Steam the fresh beans until just cooked. Place under running cold water to stop them cooking.
4   Melt the margarine in a frying pan. Add the onion and garlic. Fry until browned.
5   Add the rice and fry for a further minute.
6   Add the stock, wine and water. Bring to the boil then simmer for 15 minutes, stirring regularly. Add the mushrooms and cook until the stock is absorbed and the rice is tender.
7   Add the yams or kumara, beans and cheese. Stir gently to avoid the vegetables breaking. Cook until the vegetables are heated through and the cheese has melted.
8   Serve immediately. Crack over the pepper. Serve with a salad.

Nutrition Information (per serve) not including a salad side dish

Energy: 1972 kj (472 cal)   Carbohydrate: 76 g   Fibre: 6.2 g   Total fat: 6.4 g   Saturated fat: 2.6 g   Sodium: 1186 mg   GI: Medium
GF* Use GF stock and cheese slices.

Moroccan Pilau Rice

Basmati rice has a lower glycaemic index compared to most white rices. The rice grains tend to stay intact and they don't stick together as much as ordinary rice. It has also a lovely aromatic flavour.

2 serves	4 serves	ingredients
½ medium	1 medium	red onion
1 tablespoon	2 tablespoons	pistachios
1 tablespoon	2 tablespoons	pine nuts
½ teaspoon	1 teaspoon	vegetable oil
½ teaspoon	1 teaspoon	crushed garlic
½ – 1 teaspoon	1 – 2 teaspoons	ground allspice
⅓ cup & 1T	¾ cup	basmati rice
1 small	1 large	cinnamon stick
2	4	cardamom pods
½ cup & 2T	1¼ cups	liquid vegetable stock
½ cup	1 cup	cold water
6	12	dried apricots
¼ cup	½ cup	dried currants

1. Dice the onion.
2. Place the nuts in a non–stick frying pan and cook over a low heat until lightly browned. Remove from the pan.
3. Add the oil to the frying pan and when hot add the onion, garlic and allspice. Cook for a couple of minutes.
4. Stir through the rice. Add the cinnamon stick, cardamom pods, stock and water. Bring to the boil and then simmer, stirring occasionally, for 12 minutes.
5. Meanwhile slice the apricots into long thin slices.
6. Add the apricots and currants to the rice and stir through gently.
7. Turn the element off and cover the pan with a lid. Leave for 2 minutes or until the liquid has absorbed. Remove the cinnamon stick and cardamom pods. Stir through the nuts and serve.

Nutrition Information (per serve)

Energy: 1238 kj (297 cal)   Carbohydrate: 53 g   Fibre: 3.2 g   Total fat: 6.7 g   Saturated fat: 1.1 g   Sodium: 440 mg   GI: Low
GF* Use GF spices and vegetable stock.

Vegetable & Chickpea Fried Rice

Fried rice can be high in fat if a large amount of oil is used to keep the rice grains from sticking.
A parboiled rice is perfect for making fried rice as it does not stick together.

2 serves	4 serves	ingredients
1½ cups	3 cups	cold water
½ cup	1 cup	parboiled rice
1 small	2 small	egg/s
¼ cup	½ cup	low fat milk
½ medium	1 medium	red onion
1 small	2 small	zucchini
2 teaspoons	4 teaspoons	olive oil
1 – 1½ teaspoons	2 – 3 teaspoons	crushed garlic
½ – 1 teaspoon	1 – 2 teaspoons	crushed ginger
¼ cup	½ cup	diced red pepper
¼ cup	½ cup	broccoli florets
½ cup	1 cup	frozen mixed vegetables
½ cup	1 cup	canned chickpeas
2 tablespoons	4 tablespoons	soy sauce

1   Place the water in a pan and bring to the boil. Add the rice and cook for 10 – 15 minutes or until cooked. Drain and rinse. Refrigerate for at least 1 hour.
2   Beat the egg/s and milk lightly.
3   Preheat a non–stick wok over a low heat. Pour in the egg mixture and tilt to spread the mixture out thinly. Cook until set, remove and leave to cool. Slice into strips 1 cm by 5 cm.
4   Dice the onion and slice the zucchini into small rounds. Heat the oil in the wok and add the onion, zucchini, garlic, ginger, red pepper and broccoli. Cook, over a medium heat until the vegetables are just tender.
5   Add the rice, mixed vegetables, drained chickpeas and soy sauce. Stir continuously until the rice and the mixed vegetables are heated through. Add the chopped egg and continue to cook, stirring gently, for a further minute.
6   Serve immediately.

Nutrition Information (per serve)

Energy: 1561 kj (374 cal)   Carbohydrate: 57 g   Fibre: 5.6 g   Total fat: 10.5 g   Saturated fat: 2 g   Sodium: 470 mg   GI: Low
GF* Use GF soy sauce.

Fragrant Rice

This rice has a lovely fragrant flavour. The fresher your spices are the more fragrant they will be.

2 serves	4 serves	ingredients
½ medium	1 medium	onion
¾ teaspoon	1½ teaspoons	reduced fat (<56% fat) polyunsaturated margarine
½ teaspoon	1 teaspoon	crushed garlic
pinch	¼ teaspoon	ground cinnamon
¼ teaspoon	½ teaspoon	ground turmeric
½ teaspoon	1 teaspoon	curry powder
⅓ cup	⅔ cup	liquid chicken or vegetable stock
½ tablespoon	1 tablespoon	brown sugar
⅓ cup	⅔ cup	basmati or parboiled rice
½ cup	1 cup	creamy coconut flavoured light evaporated milk
¼ cup	½ cup	cold water
3 tablespoons	6 tablespoons	sultanas

1   Preheat the oven to 150°C (130°C fan).
2   Slice the onion finely.
3   Melt the margarine in a frying pan and add the garlic, cinnamon, turmeric and curry. Cook for 1 minute. Add the onion and cook for a further minute.
4   Add the remaining ingredients and bring to the boil.
5   Place in a covered ovenproof dish and bake for 20 – 40 minutes or until the liquid is absorbed and the rice is cooked.

Nutrition Information (per serve)

Energy: 1183 kj (284 cal)   **Carbohydrate:** 53 g   **Fibre:** 1.5 g   **Total fat:** 2.4 g   **Saturated fat:** 1.0 g   **Sodium:** 302 mg   **GI:** Low
GF* Use GF spices, curry powder, stock and evaporated milk.

pies, pastries & pizza

Corn, Bacon & Vegetable Bread Cases pg 69

Healthy Sausage Rolls pg 76

Pizzas pgs 64, 66 & 67

The smell of pies are so tempting but often disappointing when you are left with a greasy mouth and a great weight in your tummy. NOSH pies are great – even a typical kiwi bloke raved about them. The pies have a lighter and healthier pastry, than most pies, and they encapsulate a flavoursome filling. You do not need sauce with these pies!

The pie fillings and the pies can be made ahead of time, cooled quickly and then frozen in airtight containers. Leave to thaw in the refrigerator and not on the bench. Always reheat pies until they are very hot in the centre and eat while hot. Only reheat once.

NOSH frittatas, bread cases and quiches do not rely on cheese for flavour and they include vegetables. Cooking them in different shapes brings them out of the 80s into the 21st century. If you are not into eggs then don't avoid these recipes – they do not taste very eggy.

Homemade pizza – it's hard to beat, and worth the effort. To save some time, make up a large quantity of dough. Roll it out to form bases and then freeze. Bring them straight out of the freezer, sprinkle over the toppings and then cook. Allow another 5 – 10 minutes for cooking.

Bread Style Pizza Dough

This is a great pizza base and it isn't too heavy with the wholemeal flour and oat bran. If you have a microwave, try rising the dough in it. It's very simple and quick.

8 serves

ingredients	
1½ cups	plain flour
1 cup	wholemeal flour
2 tablespoons	gluten flour
½ cup	oat bran
1 teaspoon	iodised salt
1½ teaspoons	active dry yeast
1 cup	lukewarm water
1 tablespoon	olive oil

1 Combine the flours, oat bran and salt.
2 Dissolve the yeast in the lukewarm water. Add to the dry ingredients along with the oil and mix. Add extra water if needed to form a soft dough.
3 Knead for 10 minutes until smooth and elastic.
4 Cover with cling film and leave in a warm place until doubled in size (1 – 1½ hours). Alternatively, place the dough in a microwave safe bowl and cover with cling film. Place in the microwave and cook for 1 minute on low and then leave to rest for 10 minutes. Repeat the 1 minute on low and 10 minutes resting until the dough has doubled in size (40 – 50 minutes).
5 Roll and cut out to desired shape/s.

Nutrition Information (per serve)

Energy: 718 kj (172 cal) Carbohydrate: 31 g Fibre: 3.6 g Total fat: 2.8 g Saturated fat: 0.4 g Sodium: 293 mg GI: Medium

Caramelised Red Onion Jam

This jam is not only delicious on pizzas but is equally as good served warm with, venison or beef medallions, or sausages and mash.

1½ cups

ingredients	
2 cups	chopped red onions
¼ cup	no added sugar apple juice
¼ cup	medium red wine
2 tablespoons	balsamic vinegar
2 tablespoons	lightly packed brown sugar

1 Place the onions, juice, wine, vinegar and sugar into a pan. Simmer, stirring occasionally, for 20 – 30 minutes until the onions are well cooked and the liquid has gone thick and syrupy.
2 Leave to cool. Store in an airtight container, in the refrigerator.

Nutrition Information (per 2 tablespoons)

Energy: 101 kj (24 cal) Carbohydrate: 4.5 g Fibre: 0.7 g Total fat: 0.06 g Saturated fat: 0.01 g Sodium: 2 mg GI: Low GF* No modifications are necessary.

Smoked Salmon, Ricotta & Hummus Pizza

For a thin crispy pizza base, place the uncooked pizza onto a hot oven tray or for a thicker base place on a cold tray. Left over slices of pizza can be frozen in cling film and then reheated in the microwave.

	8 serves	ingredients
	1 x quantity	Bread Style Pizza Dough (page 63)
	1 x quantity	Caramelised Red Onion Jam (page 63)
Salmon Topping	100 grams	cold smoked salmon
	½ medium	red pepper
	12	black olives
	3 tablespoons	(8% fat) ricotta cheese
	5 tablespoons	hummus
	1 cup	torn and lightly packed spinach
	2 tablespoons	capers
	2 tablespoons	pine nuts
	2 tablespoons	chopped fresh coriander (optional)
	1 cup	grated mozzarella cheese

1 **Bread Dough and Caramelised Red Onion Jam:** Make according to the recipes on page 63.
2 **Salmon Topping:** Chop the salmon into chunks and the red pepper into cubes. Remove the stones from the olives and chop in half. Mix together the ricotta and hummus.
3 **Pizza Assembly:** Preheat the oven to 200°C (180°C fan).
4 Remove the dough from the bowl and knead gently for 2 minutes. Roll out thinly onto a floured surface. Cut into eight, 12 cm rounds, for individual pizzas or a 30 cm round for one large pizza.
5 Place the pizza/s onto baking paper. Spread with the onion jam, then place the spinach over the jam. Dot with the hummus mixture then sprinkle over the salmon, red pepper, olives, capers, pine nuts, coriander and cheese.
6 Place on a hot oven tray for a thin base or a cold oven tray for a thicker base.
7 For the individual pizzas, bake for 20 minutes. For the 30 cm round pizza, bake for 20 minutes then reduce the heat to 180°C (160°C fan) and cook for another 10 – 15 minutes or until cooked. If the topping is browning too quickly, cover with foil during the cooking process.
8 Serve warm.

Nutrition Information (per serve)

Energy: 1272 kj (304 cal) Carbohydrate: 39 g Fibre: 5.0 g Total fat: 9.0 g Saturated fat: 3.0 g Sodium: 726 mg GI: Medium
GF* Use GF ricotta and hummus. Use a GF pizza base or cut circles out of GF bread. Adjust cooking time.

Traditional Style Pizza with a Scone Base pg 67 (left front), Roasted Vegetable & Caramelised Onion Pizza pg 66 (right) and Smoked Salmon, Ricotta & Hummus Pizza (back)

Roasted Vegetable & Caramelised Onion Pizza

The caramelised onion jam adds a delicious flavour and moistness to this pizza.

8 serves	ingredients
1 x quantity	Bread Style Pizza Dough (page 63)
1 x quantity	Caramelised Red Onion Jam (page 63)
Roast Vegetable Topping — 6 medium	yams
4 cloves	garlic
1⅓ cups	cubed orange kumara
⅔ cup	cubed parsnip
light spray	oil
1 medium	red pepper
4 medium	mushrooms
¼ cup	cashews
1 cup	grated mozzarella cheese
¼ – ½ cup	chopped fresh herbs (optional)

1   **Bread Dough and Caramelised Red Onion Jam:** Make according to the recipes on page 63.
2   **Roast Vegetable Topping:** Preheat the oven to 200°C (180°C fan). Chop the yams into rounds.
3   Peel the garlic and slice finely. Place the yams, kumara and parsnip in a pan. Cover with water, bring to the boil and then simmer for 5 minutes.
4   Drain and place on a tray, lined with baking paper. Scatter over the garlic and spray with oil. Bake for 20 – 30 minutes until cooked and browned.
5   Chop the red pepper and mushrooms into chunks and mix through the roasted vegetables.
6   **Pizza Assembly:** Preheat the oven to 200°C (180°C fan).
7   Remove the dough from the bowl and knead gently for 2 minutes. Roll out thinly onto a floured surface. Cut into eight, 12 cm rounds, for individual pizzas or a 30 cm round for one large pizza.
8   Place the pizza/s onto baking paper. Spread the onion jam over the pizza/s and then sprinkle over the roast vegetables, cashews, cheese and herbs.
9   Place on a hot oven tray for a thin base or a cold oven tray for a thicker base.
10 For the individual pizzas, bake for 20 minutes. For the 30 cm round pizza, bake for 20 minutes then reduce the heat to 180°C (160°C fan) and cook for another 10 – 15 minutes or until cooked. If the topping is browning too quickly, cover with aluminium foil. Serve warm.

Nutrition Information (per serve)

Energy: 1359 kj (325 cal)   Carbohydrate: 49 g   Fibre: 6.5 g   Total fat: 8.1 g   Saturated fat: 2.7 g   Sodium: 389 mg   GI: Medium

GF* Use a GF pizza base or cut circles out of GF bread. Adjust cooking time.

Traditional Style Pizza with a Scone Base

This scone dough is a quick and delicious way of creating a base for a pizza. Don't substitute the buttermilk with ordinary milk – the buttermilk is there to help tenderise the mixture.

	8 serves	ingredients
Scone Base	1 ¼ cups	plain flour
	½ cup	oat bran
	½ teaspoon	baking soda
	1 tablespoon	olive oil
	½ – ⅔ cup	buttermilk
Topping	3 rashers	lean bacon
	1 medium	red onion
	½ medium	red pepper
	4	button mushrooms
	1 x 225 gram can	pineapple pieces, in natural juice
	⅔ cup	tomato relish
	¼ cup	fresh chopped herbs
	1 cup	grated mozzarella cheese

1. **Scone Base:** Combine the flour, oat bran and baking soda. Add the oil and the buttermilk until a soft dough is formed.
2. Wrap in cling film and leave to rest in the refrigerator for at least 30 minutes.
3. **Topping:** Chop the bacon, onion, red pepper and mushrooms into small pieces. Lightly fry in a non–stick pan.
4. Drain the pineapple and chop into smaller pieces.
5. **Pizza Assembly:** Preheat the oven to 200°C (180°C fan).
6. Roll the scone base out thinly. Cut into eight, 12 cm rounds, for individual pizzas or a 30 cm round for 1 large pizza. Place on greased oven tray/s.
7. Spread the relish over the base/s. Sprinkle the bacon mixture then pineapple, herbs and cheese over the base.
8. For the individual pizzas, bake for 15 – 20 minutes and the 30 cm round pizza, bake for 20 – 25 minutes or until cooked and browned. Serve warm.

Nutrition Information (per serve)

Energy: 799 kj (191 cal) **Carbohydrate:** 26 g **Fibre:** 2.4 g **Total fat:** 5.5 g **Saturated fat:** 2.4 g **Sodium:** 309 mg **GI:** Medium
GF* Use GF relish. Use a GF pizza base or cut circles out of GF bread. Adjust cooking time.

Delicious Corn, Bacon & Vegetable Bread Cases

Bread makes a quick and a low fat pastry alternative. The thinner it is rolled, the more pastry–like it becomes.

	2 serves	4 serves	ingredients
Bread Cases	4	8	thin slices wholegrain bread
	light spray	light spray	oil
Filling	¼ medium	½ medium	red onion
	1 rasher	2 rashers	lean bacon
	¼ small	½ small	red pepper
	1 medium	2 medium	whole egg/s
	½ small	1 small	zucchini
	⅓ cup	⅔ cup	canned cream style corn
	2 tablespoons	¼ cup	low fat cottage cheese
	2 tablespoons	¼ cup	grated tasty cheese
	1 teaspoon	2 teaspoons	French onion soup powder
	sprinkle	sprinkle	ground pepper
	4	8	cherry tomatoes
or	½	1	medium tomato

1　**Bread Cases:** Preheat the oven to 150°C (130°C fan). Lightly grease 4 – 8 large (¾ cup) muffin tins.
2　Remove the crusts from the bread. Using a rolling pin, roll each slice of bread until it is very thin. Place the bread into the tins, moulding it to fit the bottoms and sides. Spray lightly with oil.
3　Bake for 15 minutes. Remove from the oven and leave to cool. Increase the oven temperature to 180°C (160°C fan).
4　**Filling:** Slice the onion, bacon and red pepper finely. Fry in a non–stick frying pan until cooked.
5　Beat the egg/s gently. Grate the zucchini and add to the egg/s along with the onion mixture, corn, cottage and tasty cheeses, soup powder and ground pepper. Mix well.
6　Spoon into the bread cases, leaving a 1 cm gap from the top. Top with a whole cherry tomato or cut the whole tomato into wedges and place 1 wedge on top of each bread case.
7　Bake for 15 – 20 minutes until the egg mixture is set and browned. Serve warm or hot.

Nutrition Information (per serve)

Energy: 1139 kj (272 cal)　Carbohydrate: 34 g　Fibre: 6.0 g　Total fat: 8.5 g　Saturated fat: 2.8 g　Sodium: 636 mg　GI: Low
GF* Spread the topping onto toasted GF bread and adjust cooking time. Use GF cream style corn, cottage cheese and soup powder.

Smoky Pumpkin & Vegetable Slice

This slice is made into individual rounds and looks great. The smoked paprika gives this slice a fantastic smoky flavour. It is a great ingredient to have in your pantry.

2 serves	4 serves	ingredients
¼ cup	½ cup	uncooked brown rice
¾ cup	1½ cups	cold water
¾ cup	1½ cups	chopped pumpkin
¼ small	½ small	leek
½ small	1 small	red pepper
½ cup	1 cup	frozen corn kernels
1 teaspoon	2 teaspoons	crushed garlic
½ cup	1 cup	broccoli florets
1 medium	2 medium	whole egg/s
1 medium	2 medium	egg white/s
¼ cup	½ cup	low fat milk
¾ teaspoon	1½ teaspoons	curry powder
½ teaspoon	1 teaspoon	smoked paprika powder
½ teaspoon	1 teaspoon	chicken or vegetable stock powder
25 grams	50 grams	feta cheese
¼ cup	½ cup	chopped fresh coriander
sprinkle	sprinkle	grated parmesan cheese
sprinkle	sprinkle	pumpkin seeds

1 Place the rice and water in a pan. Bring to the boil then simmer for 25 – 35 minutes until the rice is just cooked. Rinse under cold water and leave to drain.

2 Preheat the oven to 180°C (160°C fan). Lightly grease 2 – 4 (¾ cup) ramekin dishes or muffin tins.

3 Place the pumpkin in a pan and cover with water. Cook until tender, drain and mash.

4 Chop the leek into fine rings and the red pepper into cubes. Place in a frying pan along with the corn and garlic. Fry for 2 minutes. Take off the heat and add the broccoli.

5 Combine the pumpkin, eggs, milk, curry, paprika and stock in a bowl and beat until smooth.

6 Crumble the feta cheese and stir through along with the rice, cooked vegetables and coriander. Place in the ramekins or muffin tins. Sprinkle over the cheese and seeds.

7 Bake for 30 – 40 minutes or until cooked and browned.

Nutrition Information (per serve)

Energy: 1248 kj (299 cal) Carbohydrate: 35 g Fibre: 5.2 g Total fat: 10.8 g Saturated fat: 3.9 g Sodium: 534 mg GI: Medium
GF* Use GF curry powder, smoked paprika and stock powder.

Kumara, Ham & Pineapple Frittata

This frittata would look nothing if it was made in a normal frittata shape. The height and the layering make it look like a terrine that is colourful and tasty.

4 serves	ingredients
2 medium	orange kumara
2	spring onions
1 medium	red pepper
3 slices	lean ham or bacon
⅔ cup	canned crushed pineapple, in natural juice
2 cups	torn and lightly packed spinach
2 medium	whole eggs
2 medium	egg whites
1 cup	reduced fat evaporated milk
3 tablespoons	whole seed mustard
1 teaspoon	crushed garlic
1½ tablespoons	French onion soup powder
2 tablespoons	grated parmesan cheese

1. Preheat the oven to 180°C (160°C fan). Line a loaf tin (13 x 23 cm) with baking paper.
2. Scrub the kumara and slice thinly into rounds. Place in a pan and cover with water. Bring to the boil and then simmer until just tender. Drain.
3. Chop the onions, red pepper and ham or bacon into chunks. Fry in a non–stick frying pan until the onion has browned. Drain the pineapple.
4. Place one third of the kumara slices into the bottom of the loaf tin. Place half of the spinach, onion mixture and pineapple over the kumara. Continue the layers ending with the kumara.
5. Lightly beat the eggs with the milk, mustard, garlic and soup powder. Pour over the layered kumara and sprinkle with the parmesan.
6. Bake for 45 minutes then cover with aluminium foil and bake for another 15 – 20 minutes until cooked and set. Leave in the tin for 10 minutes before removing. Serve warm.

Nutrition Information (per serve)

Energy: 1193 kj (285 cal) **Carbohydrate:** 35 g **Fibre:** 3.0 g **Total fat:** 8.7 g **Saturated fat:** 2.5 g **Sodium:** 478 mg **GI:** Low
GF* Use GF evaporated milk, whole seed mustard and soup powder.

Thai Chicken Pies pg 74 (back left), Bolognese Mince Potato Topped Pies pg 75 (middle) and Beef Hotpot Pies (front right)

Beef Hotpot Pies

These are not your typical steak pies but rather a gourmet version that are big on flavour. These are made in large muffin tins to form a tall pie which looks more trendy than a traditional pie shape.

4 serves	ingredients	4 serves	ingredients
	Ricotta Pastry:	1 x 400 gram can	chopped tomatoes, in
1 x quantity	Ricotta pastry recipe (page 74)		tomato juice
	Filling:	¼ cup	dry red wine
200 grams	lean blade steak	1 tablespoon	balsamic vinegar
½ medium	onion	1 teaspoon	lightly packed brown sugar
¼ medium	red pepper	2 teaspoons	cornflour
4 medium	mushrooms	2 tablespoons	cold water
1 teaspoon	crushed garlic	¼ cup	frozen green beans
1 teaspoon	beef stock powder		Glaze:
1 tablespoon	no added salt tomato paste	1 medium	egg
2 tablespoons	Worcestershire sauce	¼ cup	low fat milk
½ teaspoon	dried oregano or basil	sprinkle	black or white sesame seeds

1   **Ricotta Pastry:** Make the pastry according to the recipe on page 74.

2   **Filling:** Preheat the oven to 170°C (150°C fan). Trim any fat from the meat. Dice the meat, onion, red pepper and mushrooms into 1.5 cm cubes.

3   Heat a non–stick frying pan. Add the meat, onion, pepper, mushrooms and garlic and fry until the meat is browned. Place in an ovenproof dish.

4   Combine the stock, paste, Worcestershire sauce, herbs, tomatoes, wine, vinegar and sugar.

5   Pour the sauce mixture over the meat and stir through. Cover and bake for 1½ hours. Remove from the oven.

6   Mix the cornflour and water to a paste. Stir through the filling until it thickens. Add the beans and leave to cool.

7   **Assembly of Pies:** Preheat the oven to 200°C (180°C fan). Lightly grease 4 (¾ cup) muffin tins.

8   Roll the pastry out thinly. Cut out shapes to fit the bottom and sides of the tins. Place into the tins then add the cooled filling, leaving a 1 cm gap from the top of the pastry.

9   Cut out pastry shapes to fit the tops. Place on top of the beef and pinch the pastry edges together.

10 **Glaze:** Beat the egg with the low fat milk. Lightly brush the tops of the pies. Sprinkle over the seeds. Bake for 20 – 30 minutes until browned and cooked.

Nutrition Information (per serve)

Energy: 1809 kj (433 cal)   Carbohydrate: 50 g   Fibre: 4.6 g   Total fat: 14.2 g   Saturated fat: 5.3 g   Sodium: 736 mg   GI: Medium

Thai Chicken Pies

These delicious pies are made with a low fat ricotta pastry which tends to be more like a thin bread crust than a flaky pastry. Roll it out thinly to get a crisper pastry.

4 serves	ingredients	4 serves	ingredients
	Ricotta Pastry:	½ medium	red pepper
1 ½ cups	plain flour	½ cup	chopped leek
2 teaspoons	baking powder	1 ½ teaspoons	red curry paste
2 pinches	iodised salt	½ teaspoon	chicken stock powder
½ cup	oat bran	½ cup	creamy coconut flavoured
⅔ cup	(8% fat) ricotta cheese		light evaporated milk
1 medium	egg	½ cup	lightly packed spinach
1 tablespoon	olive oil	1 teaspoon	cornflour
¼ – ½ cup	buttermilk	2 teaspoons	low fat milk
	Filling:		Glaze:
½ medium	orange kumara	1 medium	egg
200 grams	fresh skinless and boneless	¼ cup	low fat milk
	chicken breasts	sprinkle	black or white sesame seeds

1 **Ricotta Pastry:** Sift the flour, baking powder and salt. Add the oat bran, ricotta, egg, oil and enough buttermilk to form a soft dough. Cover and place in the refrigerator for 30 minutes.
2 **Filling:** Scrub the kumara and dice. Boil until tender and then drain.
3 Remove any fat from the chicken and dice into 1.5 cm cubes.
4 Dice the red pepper into small cubes. Lightly fry the chicken, red pepper, leeks and curry paste in a non–stick frying pan until the chicken changes colour. Add the stock and evaporated milk. Simmer until the chicken is just cooked. Add the spinach and cook for 1 minute.
5 Dissolve the cornflour in the first measure of low fat milk. Add to the chicken and stir over the heat until thickened. Remove from the heat and leave to cool.
6 **Assembly of Pies:** Preheat the oven to 200°C (180°C fan). Lightly grease 4 (½ cup) mini loaf tins or muffin tins.
7 Roll the pastry out thinly. Cut out shapes to fit the bottom and sides of the tins. Place into the tins then add the cooled filling, leaving a 1 cm gap from the top of the pastry.
8 Cut out pastry shapes to fit the tops. Place on top of the chicken and pinch the pastry edges together.
9 **Glaze:** Beat the egg with the second measure of low fat milk. Brush the tops of the pies. Sprinkle over the seeds.
10 Bake for 20 – 30 minutes until browned and cooked.

Nutrition Information (per serve)

Energy: 1521 kj (365 cal) Carbohydrate: 43 g Fibre: 3.8 g Total fat: 9.4 g Saturated fat: 3.4 g Sodium: 459 mg GI: Medium

Bolognese Mince Potato Topped Pies

Most pies are high in fat – with most of the fat coming from the pastry. One way to reduce the fat, in pies, is to replace the top layer of pastry with a vegetable mash.

4 serves	ingredients	4 serves	ingredients
	Olive Oil Pastry:	½ cup	canned kidney beans
1 cup	plain flour	2 cups	tomato pasta sauce
⅛ teaspoon	iodised salt	2 tablespoons	Worcestershire sauce
¼ cup	oat bran	½ cup	dry red wine
1 ½ tablespoons	olive oil	½ cup	frozen peas
½ cup	cold water		Topping:
	Filling:	4 small	potatoes
1 medium	onion	to taste	iodised salt
400 grams	lean topside mince	to taste	ground pepper
1 cup	diced carrots	as required	low fat milk
1 cup	diced zucchini	sprinkle	grated parmesan cheese

1   **Olive Oil Pastry:** Sift the flour and salt. Add the oat bran, oil and water. Mix until combined and knead gently for 1 minute. Cover and place in the refrigerator for 30 minutes.

2   **Filling:** Dice the onion into small cubes. Place in a non–stick frying pan with the mince and fry until browned.

3   Add the carrot, zucchini, drained kidney beans, tomato pasta and Worcestershire sauces and wine. Simmer for 10 – 15 minutes until the sauce thickens.

4   Remove from the heat, add the peas and leave to cool.

5   **Topping:** Peel the potatoes, cut into small pieces and boil until soft. Drain. Add a small amount of salt, pepper and enough milk to make a soft mash.

6   **Assembly of Pies:** Preheat the oven to 200°C (180°C fan). Lightly grease 4 (¾ cup) pie or muffin tins. Roll the pastry out thinly. Cut to fit the bottom and sides of the tins.

7   Place the cooled mince into the tins, leaving a 1 cm gap from the top of the pastry.

8   Spread the mashed potato over the pies and sprinkle with parmesan. To stop the potato drying out, cover with aluminium foil.

9   Bake for 20 – 30 minutes until the pastry is cooked and the filling and topping are hot.

Nutrition Information (per serve)

Energy: 2216 kj (530 cal)   Carbohydrate: 59 g   Fibre: 8.6 g   Total fat: 13.4 g   Saturated fat: 4.0 g   Sodium: 560 mg   GI: Medium

Healthy Sausage Rolls

These sausage rolls only have 20% of the fat of traditional sausage rolls. This recipe uses filo pastry, instead of flaky pastry, which is much lower in fat, provided that only small amounts of oil are used between the layers.

	3 serves	6 serves	ingredients
Filling	½ medium	1 medium	red onion
	½ medium	1 medium	carrot
	½ x 300 gram can	1 x 300 gram can	kidney beans
	90 grams	175 grams	reduced fat (<13% fat) uncooked sausages
	100 grams	200 grams	lean mince such as premium or topside
	1 tablespoon	2 tablespoons	chopped spring onion or chives
	1 teaspoon	2 teaspoons	crushed garlic
	½ teaspoon	1 teaspoon	coriander seeds
	1 tablespoon	2 tablespoons	Worcestershire sauce
	½ teaspoon	1 teaspoon	curry powder
Pastry	2 sheets	4 sheets	filo pastry
	light spray	light spray	oil
	sprinkle	sprinkle	sesame or poppy seeds

1   Preheat the oven to 200°C (180°C fan). Place a layer of baking paper onto a tray.
2   **Filling:** Dice the red onion. Leaving the skin on the carrot, grate finely. Place the kidney beans into a sieve, rinse under cold water and drain. Place half of them into a bowl and mash until they are broken down into smaller pieces.
3   Remove the sausage/s from the skins and add to the mashed beans.
4   Mix through the red onion, carrot, remaining beans, mince, spring onion or chives, garlic, coriander, Worcestershire sauce and curry.
5   **Pastry and Assembling:** Place 2 sheets of filo together, spraying oil between the layers. Along the long edge, place all (3 serves) or half (6 serves) of the sausage mixture in a long strip. Roll up from the long edge.
6   Spray with oil and sprinkle with the seeds. Chop into 3 large or 6 small rolls. Repeat the process with the remaining pastry and meat, for the 6 serves.
7   Place on the tray and bake for 20 – 30 minutes or until cooked and browned.
8   Best eaten hot from the oven so that the pastry is crisp. Can be frozen and then reheated in a hot oven.

Nutrition Information (per serve)
Energy: 883 kj (211 cal)   Carbohydrate: 18 g   Fibre: 4.1 g   Total fat: 7.7 g   Saturated fat: 1.7 g   Sodium: 333 mg   GI: Low

red meat, fish & chicken

Chicken Parcels with Feta & Bacon pg 95

Potato Topped Fish Pie pg 100

Mediterranean Fish Spirals pg 99

Red meat, pork and chicken, can be part of a healthy diet if it is lean and the portion size is small. For most adults this is around 100 – 150 grams per day. This is basically the size of your palm, not including your fingers and the thickness of your smallest finger. If you feel cheated by the quantity – extend the meat with lots of vegetables or add legumes (kidney beans, chickpeas, lentils, baked beans etc). This will make your meat portion look bigger.

Fish is a great alternative to meat as it is low in saturated fat and the fat it contains is good for the heart. Try to eat fish at least 2 times a week – but not deep fried!

Aim to have at least 1 meatless meal a week. Including meatless meals will help decrease the saturated fat in your diet, providing that you do not replace it with dishes that have lots of eggs and cheese. It is also a good way of eating more vegetables and legumes.

Sausage & Kumara Bake

Sausages, even the lower fat ones, still contain more fat than lean meats. A good way of using sausages is to add them to a vegetable casserole, bean stew or risotto. This way you only need 1½ sausages per person.

	2 serves	4 serves	ingredients
Base	¼ medium	½ medium	leek
	½ medium	1 medium	red pepper
	1 cup	2 cups	chopped yams or carrots
	½ cup	1 cup	liquid beef stock
	1 teaspoon	2 teaspoons	crushed garlic
	1 tablespoon	2 tablespoons	Worcestershire sauce
	¾ cup	1½ cups	canned chopped tomatoes, in tomato juice
	¼ cup	½ cup	dry red wine
	1 tablespoon	2 tablespoons	balsamic vinegar
	1 teaspoon	2 teaspoons	lightly packed brown sugar
	3	6	reduced fat (<13% fat) beef sausages
Topping	2 medium	4 medium	potatoes
	½ medium	1 medium	orange kumara
	small sprinkle	small sprinkle	iodised salt and ground pepper
	as required	as required	low fat milk
	sprinkle	sprinkle	black sesame seeds (optional)
	1 tablespoon	2 tablespoons	grated parmesan cheese

1. **Sausage and Vegetable Base:** Preheat the oven to 160°C (140°C fan).
2. Chop the leek and red pepper into chunks.
3. In a non–stick frying pan fry the leek and red pepper for 2 minutes. Add the yams or carrots, stock, garlic, Worcestershire sauce, tomatoes, wine, vinegar and sugar. Place the sausages in an ovenproof dish, then pour over the sauce mixture. Cover and bake for 1 hour.
4. Remove from the oven. Chop each sausage into 6 rounds. Stir through the mixture.
5. Drain the sauce from the vegetable and sausage mixture into a pan.
6. Boil until thick and syrupy. Pour over the vegetable and sausage mixture and gently stir through.
7. **Topping:** Peel the potatoes and kumara. Boil until soft. Drain. Season with salt and pepper.
8. Mash the potatoes and kumara with enough milk to make a soft mash.
9. Spread over the vegetable and sausage mixture and sprinkle with the sesame seeds and cheese.
10. Bake at 200°C (180°C fan) for 10 – 20 minutes until heated through and browned.

Nutrition Information (per serve)

Energy: 2055 kj (489 cal) Carbohydrate: 64 g Fibre: 5.5 g Total fat: 13.8 g Saturated fat: 3.3 g Sodium: 1259 mg GI: Low
GF* Use GF stock, Worcestershire sauce, canned tomatoes and sausages.

Meatballs with a Relish Sauce

Mince can be high in fat. For recipes, where you can't pre–cook the mince and drain the fat, you need to choose lean mince. These meatballs make a great meal for adults and children alike!

	2 serves	4 serves	ingredients
Meatballs	¼ medium	½ medium	red onion
	200 grams	400 grams	lean mince such as topside or premium
	1 dessertspoon	2 dessertspoons	no added salt tomato paste
	1 teaspoon	2 teaspoons	Worcestershire sauce
	½ teaspoon	1 teaspoon	crushed garlic
	½ teaspoon	1 teaspoon	ground coriander
	¼ teaspoon	½ teaspoon	dried mixed herbs
	3 tablespoons	6 tablespoons	rolled oats
	1 small	1 medium	egg white
Relish Sauce	¼ medium	½ medium	red onion
	1 tablespoon	2 tablespoons	diced green pepper
	¼ cup	½ cup	diced mushrooms or eggplant
	½ x 400 gram can	1 x 400 gram can	chopped tomatoes, in thick tomato juice
	1 teaspoon	2 teaspoons	lightly packed brown sugar
	1 tablespoon	2 tablespoons	balsamic vinegar
	¼ cup	½ cup	liquid vegetable stock
	2 cups (110 grams)	4 cups (220 grams)	uncooked pasta such as penne or spaghetti
Garnish	2	4	fresh thyme branches (optional)

1. **Meatballs:** Preheat the oven to 170°C (150°C fan).
2. Finely slice the first onion. Combine with the remaining meatball ingredients and roll into 20 (2 servings) or 40 (4 servings) small balls.
3. Place in an ovenproof dish lined with baking paper. Bake for 15 – 20 minutes or until cooked. Keep warm.
4. **Relish Sauce:** Finely slice the second onion and place it in a saucepan with the green pepper, mushrooms or eggplant, tomatoes, sugar, vinegar and stock.
5. Simmer for 10 minutes or until thickened. Stir occasionally.
6. Meanwhile cook the pasta according to the instructions on the packet. Drain.
7. Serve the meatballs on top of the pasta, spoon over the sauce and garnish. Serve with a salad.

Nutrition Information (per serve) not including a salad side dish

Energy: 1799 kj (430 cal) Carbohydrate: 49 g Fibre: 7.2 g Total fat: 9.7 g Saturated fat: 2.8 g Sodium: 807 mg GI: Low
GF* Use GF tomato paste, Worcestershire sauce, canned tomatoes and vegetable stock. Substitute the oats with GF bread crumbs and the pasta with a GF pasta.

Mini Ham Wrapped Meat Loaves

The thought of meat loaf conjures up, for me, some anaemic, unexciting looking food. These mini meat loaves wrapped in ham look like they've come out of some trendy delicatessen – and they are full of vegetables and flavour.

3 serves	6 serves	ingredients
½ cup	1 cup	canned kidney beans
½ medium	1 medium	red onion
½ medium	1 medium	carrot
2 tablespoons	¼ cup	diced red pepper or sun dried tomatoes
1 tablespoon	2 tablespoons	chopped fresh herbs such as parsley
½ teaspoon	1 teaspoon	dried mixed herbs
200 grams	400 grams	lean mince such as topside or premium
2 tablespoons	¼ cup	frozen whole kernel corn
½ teaspoon	1 teaspoon	mustard powder
1 tablespoon	2 tablespoons	tomato sauce
1 tablespoon	2 tablespoons	Worcestershire sauce
1 teaspoon	2 teaspoons	beef stock powder
¼ cup	½ cup	rolled oats
1 small	1 medium	egg white
6 slices	12 slices	shaved ham
1 tablespoon	2 tablespoons	tomato sauce
1 tablespoon	2 tablespoons	Worcestershire sauce
1 tablespoon	2 tablespoons	hot water
Garnish 3	6	fresh sage leaves (optional)

1. Preheat the oven to 180°C (160°C fan). Lightly grease 3 – 6 (½ cup) mini loaf tins.
2. Drain the kidney beans and mash. Finely slice the onion. Leaving the skin on the carrot, finely grate.
3. Add the onion, carrot, red pepper or sun dried tomatoes, herbs, mince, corn, mustard, first measure of tomato and Worcestershire sauces, stock, oats and egg to the kidney beans. Mix well.
4. Lay strips of the shaved ham in the bottom and up the sides of the tins. Lightly pack in the meat mixture and bake for 15 minutes.
5. Mix the second measure of the tomato and Worcestershire sauces and water to a smooth paste. Spread over the top of the loaves. Cook for another 10 minutes.
6. Serve upside down, garnished with sage leaves. Serve with crusty bread and a green salad.

Nutrition Information (per serve) not including bread and salad side dishes

Energy: 960 kj (230 cal) Carbohydrate: 16 g Fibre: 3.8 g Total fat: 7.7 g Saturated fat: 2.4 g Sodium: 1339 mg GI: Low
GF* Use GF mustard powder, tomato and Worcestershire sauces and stock powder. Substitute the oats with GF bread crumbs.

Beef & Sesame Stirfry

Stirfries make quick meals. It's a way of eating less meat without feeling that you have been short changed. Stirfries are also a simple way of adding lots of vegetables into your diet.

	2 serves	4 serves	ingredients
	200 grams	400 grams	lean rump steak
	1 medium	2 medium	spring onion/s
	1 medium	2 medium	red pepper/s
	1 medium	2 medium	carrot/s
	1 cup	2 cups	fresh green beans
	¾ cup	1½ cups	broccoli florets
	¾ cup	1½ cups	chopped eggplant or mushrooms
	1 – 1½ teaspoons	2 – 3 teaspoons	crushed garlic
	1 – 1½ teaspoons	2 – 3 teaspoons	crushed ginger
	2 tablespoons	4 tablespoons	dry red wine
	2 tablespoons	4 tablespoons	Worcestershire sauce
	1½ teaspoons	1 tablespoon	honey
	1 tablespoon	2 tablespoons	toasted cashews
Garnish	1 tablespoon	2 tablespoons	sesame seeds

1. Trim any fat off the meat and slice the meat into thin strips.
2. Chop the onion/s and red pepper/s into strips, carrot/s into slices and remove the ends from the beans. Steam the carrots, beans and broccoli until they are still crisp to bite.
3. Heat a non–stick wok or frying pan over a high heat. Add the red pepper, eggplant or mushrooms, garlic, ginger and meat. Stir frequently until the meat is just cooked (4 – 5 minutes).
4. Add the wine, Worcestershire sauce and honey. Cook for another 2 minutes.
5. Add the carrots, beans and broccoli and cook until heated through.
6. Stir through the onion and cashews and serve immediately over pasta or rice.
7. Sprinkle with sesame seeds.

Nutrition Information (per serve) not including pasta or rice

Energy: 1178 kj (282 cal) Carbohydrate: 16 g Fibre: 6 g Total fat: 10 g Saturated fat: 2.7 g Sodium: 270 mg GI: Low
GF* Use GF Worcestershire sauce.

Coconut Beef Curry

Coconut cream, which is high in saturated fat, is often added to curries to give them a rich flavour. Coconut milk powder is a great alternative as you only need small quantities to get a creamy coconut flavour.

2 serves	4 serves	ingredients
240 grams	480 grams	lean stewing steak
½ medium	1 medium	red onion
½ teaspoon	1 teaspoon	ground turmeric
½ teaspoon	1 teaspoon	ground cumin
½ teaspoon	1 teaspoon	ground coriander
½ teaspoon	1 teaspoon	curry powder
½ teaspoon	1 teaspoon	crushed garlic
½ teaspoon	1 teaspoon	crushed ginger
½ x 400 gram can	1 x 400 gram can	chopped tomatoes, in thick tomato juice
2 tablespoons	¼ cup	coconut milk powder
1 tablespoon	2 tablespoons	balsamic vinegar
½	1	cinnamon stick
1cm x 3cm strip	2cm x 3cm strip	lemon rind
1 teaspoon	2 teaspoons	lightly packed brown sugar
½ cup	1 cup	canned chickpeas
1 cup	2 cups	cold water
½ cup	1 cup	torn and lightly packed spinach
Garnish ¼ cup	½ cup	chopped coriander (optional)

1. Trim off any fat from the meat and dice the meat. Chop the onion.
2. Heat a non–stick frying pan then add the meat, onion, turmeric, cumin, coriander, curry, garlic and ginger. Cook for 2 minutes, stirring frequently.
3. Add the tomatoes, coconut milk powder, vinegar, cinnamon stick, lemon rind, sugar, drained chickpeas and water. Place in an ovenproof dish and cover. Marinate in the refrigerator for 1 hour.
4. Preheat the oven to 160°C (140°C fan). Bake for 1¾ – 2 hours or until cooked.
5. Add the spinach to the casserole. Bake for another 5 minutes or until wilted. Remove and discard the cinnamon stick and lemon rind. Serve over basmati rice and sprinkle with coriander.
6. Serve with a range of coloured vegetables.

Nutrition Information (per serve) not including rice and vegetable side dishes

Energy: 1220 kj (292 cal) Carbohydrate: 14 g Fibre: 3.5 g Total fat: 12.1 g Saturated fat: 6.6 g Sodium: 368 mg GI: Low
GF* Use GF turmeric, cumin, coriander, curry powder, canned tomatoes and coconut milk.

Sweet & Sour Pork

Not all cuts of pork are high in fat – choose trim pork varieties. The slow cooking of this dish brings out a stronger pork flavour.

2 serves	4 serves	ingredients
250 grams	500 grams	lean pork pieces
½ cup	1 cup	canned sliced pineapple, in natural juice
½ medium	1 medium	red onion
¼ medium	½ medium	green pepper
¼ medium	½ medium	red pepper
½ cup	1 cup	pineapple juice
1 dessertspoon	2 dessertspoons	no added salt tomato paste
½ teaspoon	1 teaspoon	crushed garlic
½ teaspoon	1 teaspoon	crushed ginger
2 teaspoons	4 teaspoons	Worcestershire sauce
½ teaspoon	1 teaspoon	beef stock powder
1 tablespoon	2 tablespoons	lightly packed brown sugar
2 teaspoons	4 teaspoons	malt or balsamic vinegar
¼ cup	½ cup	cold water

1. Preheat the oven to 160°C (140°C fan).
2. Trim any fat off the meat.
3. Drain the pineapple and reserve the juice. Chop the pineapple, onion, green and red peppers into 3 cm chunks.
4. Combine all the ingredients except the green and red peppers. Place in a covered ovenproof dish and cook for 1¼ hours.
5. Add the green and red peppers and cook for a further 15 minutes.
6. Drain the sauce from the pork and keep the pork warm. Place the sauce in a pan and cook until thick and syrupy. Stir through the pork.
7. Serve hot with basmati rice and a range of coloured vegetables.

Nutrition Information (per serve) not including rice and vegetable side dishes
Energy: 977 kj (234 cal)   Carbohydrate: 23 g   Fibre: 1.2 g   Total fat: 3.4 g   Saturated fat: 1.3 g   Sodium: 306 mg   GI: Low
GF* Use GF tomato paste, Worcestershire sauce and stock powder. Use balsamic vinegar.

Sausage & Cannelloni Bean Casserole

This casserole is a great way to incorporate beans (legumes) into the diet – and to enjoy them.
I've used canned (cooked) ones in this recipe to make it quick and easy to prepare.

	2 serves	4 serves	ingredients
	3	6	reduced fat (<13% fat) pork sausages
	1 medium	2 medium	red onion/s
	3 medium	6 medium	fresh tomatoes
or	½ x 400 gram can	1 x 400 gram can	whole tomatoes, in thick tomato juice
	½ medium	1 medium	red pepper
	1 medium	2 medium	zucchini
	2 cloves	4 cloves	garlic
	1 teaspoon	2 teaspoons	coriander seeds
	¾ cup	1½ cups	liquid beef stock
	1 tablespoon	2 tablespoons	Worcestershire sauce
	½ – 1 teaspoon	1 – 2 teaspoons	dried sage
	½ cup	1 cup	canned cannelloni beans
Garnish	2 tablespoons	¼ cup	sage leaves (optional)

1. Boil the sausages in water until just cooked. Cool then slice into thin rounds.
2. Chop the onion/s into thin wedges and the tomatoes, red pepper and zucchini into small chunks.
3. Slice the garlic cloves into small pieces. Lightly crush the coriander seeds.
4. In a non–stick frying pan cook the onion with the garlic and coriander until lightly browned.
5. Add the tomatoes, red pepper, stock, sauce and sage. Simmer for 20 minutes until the onion/s are soft.
6. Add the zucchini and cook for a further 5 minutes or until just tender.
7. Rinse the beans with cold water and drain. Add the beans and sausages to the vegetable mixture. Cook until heated through.
8. Sprinkle with sage leaves and serve with some crusty bread and a range of coloured vegetables.

Nutrition Information (per serve) not including bread and vegetable side dishes

Energy: 1349 kj (323 cal) Carbohydrate: 29 g Fibre: 7.4 g Total fat: 12.7 g Saturated fat: 2.7 g Sodium: 1293 mg GI: Low
GF* Use GF sausages, canned tomatoes, stock and Worcestershire sauce.

Fruity Stuffed Pork

Apples, apricots and prunes are great partners with pork. Instead of crushed ginger add some chopped stem ginger. For a special occasion, wrap a lean piece of bacon around the outside of these rolls.

4 serves	ingredients
1 medium	eating apple
8	dried apricots
6	dried prunes
1½ teaspoons	crushed ginger
½ cup	dry white wine
2 teaspoons	apple juice concentrate
2 teaspoons	slivered almonds
4 tablespoons	(8% fat) ricotta cheese
4 pieces	pork schnitzel

1 Preheat the oven to 180°C (160°C fan).
2 Dice the apple, apricots and prunes into small cubes.
3 Place the fruit, ginger, wine and juice in a pan. Simmer until the liquids are absorbed. Add the nuts.
4 Spread 1 tablespoon of ricotta onto one side of each of the pork slices. Place the fruit stuffing along the centre of each piece of pork. Roll up.
5 Hold together with toothpicks. Place in an ovenproof dish, cover and bake for 30 minutes or until cooked.
6 Remove the toothpicks, slice into rounds or in half diagonally.
7 Serve with a pilau rice and a range of coloured vegetables or salad.

Nutrition Information (per serving) not including rice and vegetable or salad side dishes
Energy: 948 kj (227 cal)   Carbohydrate: 14 g   Fibre: 1.9 g   Total fat: 4.9 g   Saturated fat: 2.0 g
Sodium: 84 mg   GI: Low   GF* Use GF ricotta cheese.

Pork with a Citrus & Apple Relish

Fat, in meat, gives it flavour and keeps it moist. However, we should be eating lean meats. To boost the flavour of lean meat, marinate and serve it with a relish or a low fat sauce. To keep it moist, try not to overcook it – pork is cooked when the juices are clear.

4 serves	ingredients
4 teaspoons	orange marmalade
½ cup	medium white wine
½ cup	orange juice
1 teaspoon	crushed ginger
4 teaspoons	balsamic vinegar
4 x 120 gram	lean pork steaks
2 medium	eating apples
2 tablespoons	raisins
½ cup	cold water

1 Combine the marmalade, wine, juice, ginger and vinegar. Pour over the pork, cover and refrigerate for at least 3 hours.
2 Dice the apple into small cubes. Place in a pan and add the raisins, water and marinade drained from the meat.
3 Boil, then simmer until the apple is cooked and the liquid has gone syrupy. Keep warm.
4 Heat a non–stick frying pan. Add the pork and cook until the juices run clear.
5 Serve with the apple relish, a kumara mash and a range of vegetables.

Nutrition Information (per serving) not including mash and vegetable side dishes
Energy: 938 kj (224 cal)   Carbohydrate: 17 g   Fibre: 1.1 g   Total fat: 3.4 g   Saturated fat: 1.3 g
Sodium: 108 mg   GI: Low   GF* No modifications are needed.

Tuscan Chicken

Most of the fat in chicken is found under the skin. The chicken will dry out quicker without the skin so cover it with something moist and do not overcook it.

	2 serves	4 serves	ingredients
	2 x 100 gram	4 x 100 gram	fresh boneless chicken breasts
	½ medium	1 medium	red onion
	3 medium	6 medium	mushrooms
	½ medium	1 medium	red pepper
	2 medium	4 medium	fresh tomatoes
	½ teaspoon	1 teaspoon	olive oil
	2 cloves	4 cloves	garlic
	¼ cup	½ cup	dry red wine
	1 tablespoon	2 tablespoons	balsamic vinegar
	1 tablespoon	2 tablespoons	fresh basil
or	½ teaspoon	1 teaspoon	dried basil
	8	16	black olives (optional)
Garnish	1 tablespoon	2 tablespoons	toasted pine nuts
	2 tablespoons	¼ cup	fresh basil

1 Preheat the oven to 180°C (160°C fan).
2 Remove the skin from the chicken.
3 Chop the onion into small wedges, the mushrooms into chunks, the red pepper into 2 cm cubes and the tomatoes into quarters.
4 Heat a frying pan. Add the oil, onion, mushrooms, red pepper and garlic. Lightly fry. Add the tomatoes, wine, vinegar and the first measure of basil. Cook for 5 minutes. Remove the stones from the olives and chop in half. Add to the vegetable mixture.
5 Place the chicken in an ovenproof dish and pour over the vegetable sauce. Cover and bake for 1 hour.
6 Sprinkle over the nuts and basil. Serve with potatoes and green vegetables.

Nutrition Information (per serve) not including potato and green vegetable side dishes
Energy: 953 kj (228 cal) Carbohydrate: 9 g Fibre: 3.3 g Total fat: 7.5 g Saturated fat: 1.4 g Sodium: 331 mg GI: Low
GF* No modifications needed.

NOSH: red meat, fish & chicken

Moroccan Chicken

The sauce of this recipe is cooked until it is thick and syrupy – this is called a reduction. The sauce becomes much more intense and flavoursome this way.

2 serves	4 serves	ingredients
4 small	8 small	fresh or frozen chicken drumsticks
¼ cup	½ cup	no added sugar orange juice
¼ cup	½ cup	medium white wine
½ cup	1 cup	cold water
½ teaspoon	1 teaspoon	crushed ginger
½ teaspoon	1 teaspoon	crushed garlic
¼ teaspoon	½ teaspoon	ground cinnamon
1 teaspoon	2 teaspoons	chicken stock powder
2 dessertspoons	4 dessertspoons	plum sauce
½ teaspoon	1 teaspoon	lightly packed brown sugar
Garnish sprinkle	sprinkle	sliced almonds
1 tablespoon	2 tablespoons	chopped spring onions

1. Preheat the oven to 180°C (160°C fan).
2. If the chicken is frozen, thaw. Remove the skin from the chicken and place the chicken in an ovenproof dish.
3. Combine the juice, wine, water, ginger, garlic, cinnamon, stock, plum sauce and sugar. Pour over the chicken and cover.
4. Bake for 40 minutes or until cooked.
5. Pour the juice into a frying pan and skim off the fat from the surface. Keep the chicken warm. Boil the sauce until it is thick and syrupy. Pour over the chicken.
6. Sprinkle with the almonds and spring onions.
7. Serve with rice or potatoes and a range of coloured vegetables.

Nutrition Information (per serve) not including rice or potato and vegetable side dishes

Energy: 993 kj (238 cal)   Carbohydrate: 8 g   Fibre: 0.7 g   Total fat: 7.8 g   Saturated fat: 1.8 g   Sodium: 551 mg   GI: Low
GF* Use GF stock powder, spice and plum sauce.

Chicken Parcels with Feta & Bacon

This chicken recipe is really quick and tasty. The feta cheese can be replaced with a lower fat cheese such as ricotta.

2 serves	4 serves	ingredients
2 x 100 gram	4 x 100 gram	fresh boneless chicken breasts or thighs
2 teaspoons	4 teaspoons	sun dried tomato or basil pesto
4 thin slices	8 thin slices	feta cheese
1 slice	2 slices	lean bacon

1. Preheat the oven to 180°C (160°C fan).
2. Remove the skin from the chicken.
3. Spread a teaspoon of pesto over the top of each piece of chicken.
4. Place 2 slices of feta cheese onto each piece of chicken.
5. Chop the bacon in half. Wrap it around the centre of the chicken. Hold in place with toothpicks or tie with an ovenproof string.
6. Place in an ovenproof dish. Bake for 20 – 30 minutes or until cooked.
7. Serve with oven baked potato wedges or new potatoes and a salad.

Nutrition Information (per serve) not including potato and salad side dishes

Energy: 800 kj (191 cal)   Carbohydrate: 1.1 g   Fibre: 0.1 g   Total fat: 8.3 g   Saturated fat: 2.9 g   Sodium: 559 mg   GI: Low
GF* Use GF pesto.

Asian Style Salmon

Salmon contains omega fats that are good for the heart. It is expensive to buy per kilogram, however you only need to purchase small amounts as it is quite rich.

4 serves	ingredients
4 x 120 gram	salmon fillets or steaks
2 tablespoons	Worcestershire sauce
2 tablespoons	dry white wine
1½ teaspoons	crushed ginger
2 teaspoons	honey
sprinkle	black and white sesame seeds (optional garnish)

1. Wash the salmon under cold water. Pat dry with a paper towel.
2. Place the Worcestershire sauce, wine, ginger and honey in a frying pan and cook over a medium heat until the honey is melted.
3. Add the salmon and cook for 2 minutes on each side. Remove the salmon and keep warm. Continue cooking the sauce until it has become syrupy.
4. To serve, drizzle the salmon with the sauce. Sprinkle over the sesame seeds.
5. Serve with basmati rice, bok choy and a range of coloured vegetables.

Nutrition Information (per serve) not including rice, bok choy and vegetable side dishes

Energy: 1082 kj (259 cal) Carbohydrate: 5 g Fibre: 0.1 g Total fat: 14.8 g Saturated fat: 4.5 g
Sodium: 159 mg GI: Low GF* Use GF Worcestershire sauce.

Smoked Salmon & Kumara Cakes

I love smoked salmon as it is very highly flavoured. Hot smoked salmon can be used, instead of cold smoked, however it won't look as attractive as it falls apart when it is cut and stirred through.

4 serves	ingredients
4 (600 grams)	orange kumara
4 small	spring onions
100 grams	cold smoked salmon
2 teaspoons	coriander seeds
2 teaspoons	crushed garlic
2 medium	whole eggs
2 medium	egg whites
½ cup	low fat milk
2 tablespoons	coconut milk powder
4 teaspoons	red curry paste
2 tablespoons	chopped fresh coriander

1. Scrub the kumara and chop into 1 cm cubes. Cover with water and cook until just tender. Drain. Mash a quarter of the kumara and leave the rest cubed. Leave to cool.
2. Finely slice the onions. Chop the salmon into small pieces.
3. Lightly fry the onions with the coriander seeds and garlic.
4. Beat the whole eggs, egg whites, low fat milk, coconut milk powder and curry paste together.
5. Stir through gently the mashed and cubed kumara, onion mixture and fresh coriander.
6. Heat a non–stick frying pan. Place 2 large tablespoons of the mixture together to form a cake (9 cm rounds). Turn over when bubbles appear.
7. Place in a warm oven when cooked. Repeat until the mixture is finished.
8. Serve the cakes hot, stacked on top of each other with a green leafy salad.

Nutrition Information (per serve) not including a salad side dish

Energy: 1202 kj (288 cal) Carbohydrate: 43 g Fibre: 4.8 g Total fat: 6.8 g Saturated fat: 3.2 g
Sodium: 570 mg GI: Low GF* Use GF coconut milk powder and curry paste.

Asian Style Salmon

Mediterranean Fish Spirals

White fish makes a great light meal but it can be rather bland by itself without the addition of herbs or other flavoursome ingredients. This recipe adds flavour by marinating it with pesto and serving it with a tasty vegetable mix.

	2 serves	4 serves	ingredients
	2 x 100 gram	4 x 100 gram	fresh fish fillets
	2 teaspoons	4 teaspoons	basil pesto
	2 small	4 small	zucchini
	2 cloves	4 cloves	garlic
	½ medium	1 medium	red onion
	2 medium	4 medium	whole fresh tomatoes
or	10	20	cherry tomatoes
	6	12	black olives
	1 tablespoon	2 tablespoons	balsamic vinegar
	1 teaspoon	2 teaspoons	olive oil
Garnish	2 tablespoons	¼ cup	fresh herbs such as basil

1. Spread the fish with the pesto and roll up. Secure with a toothpick. Cover and place in the refrigerator to marinate for 2 hours.
2. Preheat the oven to 200°C (180°C fan).
3. Chop the zucchini into long thin spaghetti like slices.
4. Chop the garlic into thin slices and the onion into wedges. Heat a non–stick frying pan. Add the garlic and onion and cook until lightly browned.
5. Add the zucchini and whole tomatoes chopped into wedges, or cherry tomatoes and cook for 2 minutes.
6. Remove the stones from the olives and chop in half. Sprinkle over the zucchini mixture.
7. Place the mixture in an ovenproof dish. Drizzle over the vinegar and oil and cover.
8. Place the fish in a separate covered ovenproof dish.
9. Bake both dishes together for 15 minutes or until the fish and zucchini are cooked.
10. Serve the zucchini and tomato mixture topped with the fish. Sprinkle over some fresh herbs.
11. Serve with new potatoes and a green leafy salad.

Nutrition Information (per serve) not including potato and salad side dishes

Energy: 758 kj (181 cal) Carbohydrate: 8 g Fibre: 3.6 g Total fat: 7.1 g Saturated fat: 1 g Sodium: 306 mg GI: Low
GF* Use GF pesto.

Potato Topped Fish Pie

We should all be trying to eat at least 2 fish meals a week – but not deep fried fish! Tinned fish is a relatively inexpensive way of incorporating fish into the diet.

	2 serves	4 serves	ingredients
Topping	2 medium	4 medium	potatoes
	½ medium	1 medium	red kumara
	¼ teaspoon	½ teaspoon	crushed garlic (optional)
	1 teaspoon	2 teaspoons	whole seed mustard
	as required	as required	low fat milk
	to taste	to taste	iodised salt and ground pepper
Filling	½ medium	1 medium	red onion
	2 dessertspoons	4 dessertspoons	cornflour
	1½ teaspoons	1 tablespoon	mustard powder
	½ x 375ml can	1 x 375 ml can	reduced fat evaporated milk
	100 ml	200 ml	low fat milk
	1 teaspoon	2 teaspoons	malt or balsamic vinegar
	½ teaspoon	1 teaspoon	castor sugar
	1 x 185 gram can	2 x 185 gram cans	smoked fish, in spring water
	1 medium	2 medium	hard–boiled egg/s
	2 tablespoons	¼ cup	grated parmesan cheese

1. Preheat the oven to 180°C (160°C fan).
2. **Topping:** Peel the potatoes and kumara. Boil until soft. Drain and mash with the garlic and whole seed mustard. Add enough milk to make a moist mash. Season with salt and pepper.
3. **Filling:** Slice the onion finely. Fry in a non–stick pan, over a low heat, until cooked.
4. Stir through the cornflour and mustard powder. Slowly add the evaporated milk and the second measure of low fat milk. Stir over the heat until thickened. Remove from the heat. Add the vinegar and sugar.
5. Drain the fish and flake. Chop the egg/s into chunks. Add the fish and eggs to the sauce and stir through. Place in an ovenproof dish or in individual ramekins.
6. **Assembling:** Spread the mashed potato over the fish and sprinkle with the cheese.
7. Bake for 10 – 15 minutes for the individual ramekins or 20 – 40 minutes for the larger dish until heated through and browned. Serve hot with stirfried vegetables or a green leafy salad.

Nutrition Information (per serve) not including vegetable or salad side dishes

Energy: 2004 kj (479 cal) **Carbohydrate:** 51 g **Fibre:** 3.5 g **Total fat:** 10.4 g **Saturated fat:** 4.2 g **Sodium:** 473 mg **GI:** Medium

GF* Use GF mustards, cornflour, and evaporated milk. Use balsamic vinegar instead of malt.

desserts

Not many of us can resist dessert – but then why should we when it is totally permissible. Desserts do not have to be avoided but they should be considered as treat foods – that is, eaten occasionally.

If you have to finish a meal with something sweet – choose some fruit or yoghurt. This is a way of satisfying a sweet craving without getting lots of fat and kilojoules. It is also a way of eating more fruit and including low fat dairy products in your diet.

NOSH dessert recipes are considerably lower in fat, sugar and kilojoules and higher in fibre than standard recipes. Still – this is not permission to eat dessert more frequently.

For people, with lipid disorders, keep the desserts that have a higher amount of saturated fat for very exceptional treats. If you have diabetes, and plan to include a dessert into your meal, eat less carbohydrate in your main to compensate for the extra carbohydrate that is in the dessert.

Baked Blueberry & Lemon Tart

Pastry is often high in fat. This short sweet pastry is low in fat but it still has a great texture and flavour. There is no rubbing in the fat – the food processor or mixer does it for you.

	4 serves	8 serves	ingredients
Base	1½ tablespoons	3 tablespoons	(70% fat) polyunsaturated margarine
	½ tablespoon	1 tablespoon	icing sugar
	1 teaspoon	2 teaspoons	custard powder
	¼ cup & 2T	¾ cup	plain flour
	½ teaspoon	1 teaspoon	baking powder
	½ tablespoon	1 tablespoon	ground almonds
	2 tablespoons	¼ cup	low fat milk
Filling	2 small	3 medium	whole eggs
	125 grams	250 grams	reduced fat cream cheese
	¼ cup	½ cup	castor sugar[S] or equivalent sweetener[ES]
	1½ teaspoons	1 tablespoon	grated lemon rind
	2 tablespoons	¼ cup	lemon juice
	½ cup	1 cup	reduced fat evaporated milk
	2 tablespoons	¼ cup	ground almonds
	½ cup	1 cup	fresh or frozen blueberries

1. **Base:** Line the base of a 17 cm (4 serves) or a 24 cm (8 serves) round flan tin with baking paper and lightly grease the sides.
2. In a food processor or mixer place the margarine, icing sugar, custard powder, flour, baking powder and the first measure of almonds. Mix until the mixture resembles fine breadcrumbs.
3. Add the low fat milk until the mixture is soft and combined. Refrigerate for 30 minutes.
4. Preheat the oven to 180°C (160°C fan). Roll the pastry to fit the base and sides of the tin. Prick the pastry all over with a fork. Bake for 10 minutes.
5. **Filling:** Separate the eggs. Beat the yolks with the cream cheese, sugar or sweetener, lemon rind, juice and evaporated milk until smooth. Stir through the ground almonds.
6. Beat the egg whites until thick and foamy. Fold into the cheese mixture.
7. Place the berries into the pastry case. Spread over the filling.
8. Bake for 15 – 20 minutes (4 serves) or 25 – 30 minutes (8 serves) or until firm. Leave to cool.
9. Refrigerate for at least 2 hours. Lightly dust with icing sugar to serve.

Nutrition Information (per serve)

Energy: 1119 kj (268 cal) Carbohydrate: 23 g Fibre: 1.0 g Total fat: 14.4 g Saturated fat: 5.1 g Sodium: 333 mg GI: Low
GF* Make the recipe without the pastry or make a gluten free pastry. Use GF cream cheese and evaporated milk.

Tiramisu

The Irish Cream liqueur adds a special flavour to this Tiramisu. Other liqueurs such as a coffee liqueur, rum or brandy could be used in place of the Irish Cream.

	2 serves	4 serves	ingredients
Sponge Layer	1 medium	2 medium	egg/s
	2 dessertspoons	4 dessertspoons	castor sugar
	2 tablespoons	¼ cup	cornflour
	½ teaspoon	1 teaspoon	baking powder
	2 teaspoons	4 teaspoons	instant coffee
	3 tablespoons	6 tablespoons	hot water
	1 tablespoon	2 tablespoons	Irish Cream
Filling	100 grams	200 grams	reduced fat cream cheese
	½ cup	1 cup	low fat plain yoghurt
	¼ teaspoon	½ teaspoon	vanilla essence
	½ – 1 tablespoon	1 – 2 tablespoons	castor sugar[S] or equivalent sweetener[ES]
Garnish	as required	as required	fresh cherries or cocoa

1. **Sponge:** Preheat the oven to 200°C (180°C fan). Line the base of one 20 cm round tin (2 serves) or two 20 cm round tins (4 serves) with baking paper and lightly grease the sides of the tins.
2. Beat the egg/s until thick. Add the sugar and continue beating until stiff.
3. Sift the cornflour and baking powder. Fold gently through the egg mixture until combined. Place in the tin/s and level. Bake for 10 – 15 minutes until the mixture springs back when touched.
4. Dissolve the coffee in the hot water. Stir through the liqueur.
5. **Filling:** Beat the cream cheese, yoghurt, vanilla and sugar or sweetener together until smooth.
6. **Assembling:** Using 1 cup parfait glasses, cut shapes out of the sponge to fit the bases.
   Brush the sponge with the coffee mixture until it is moistened but not soaked.
7. Place one third of the cream cheese mixture on top of the base sponge
   Cut some of the sponge to fit on top of the cream cheese mixture then brush it with coffee.
8. Place another third of the cream cheese mixture on top. Repeat with the sponge and cream layers once more.
9. Cover and refrigerate for several hours for the flavours to develop. To serve, top with fresh cherries or dust over some cocoa.

Nutrition Information (per serve)

Energy: 1292 kj (309 cal) Carbohydrate: 37 g Fibre: 0.9 g Total fat: 12 g Saturated fat: 6.0 g Sodium: 498 mg GI: Low
GF* Use GF cornflour, baking powder, cream cheese, yoghurt and cocoa.

Traditional Cheesecake

Most cheesecakes are high in fat due to the inclusion of high fat dairy products. This cheesecake uses lower fat alternatives and it is still creamy and rich tasting.

	6 serves	ingredients
Base	1 medium	whole egg
	2 dessertspoons	castor sugar
	2 tablespoons	cornflour
	½ teaspoon	baking powder
Filling	4 teaspoons	gelatine
	2 tablespoons	cold water
	½ cup	low fat and salt reduced cottage cheese
	125 grams	reduced fat cream cheese
	½ cup	sweetened Greek style yoghurt
	⅓ cup	castor sugar[S] or equivalent sweetener[ES]
	2 teaspoons	grated lemon rind
	4 teaspoons	lemon juice
Topping	1 packet	low calorie berry flavoured jelly
	1 cup	boiling water
	1 cup	fresh berries such as raspberries or cherries

1. **Base:** Preheat the oven to 200°C (180°C fan). Line the bottom and sides of a 17 cm round cake tin with baking paper. Beat the egg until thick. Add the sugar and beat until stiff.
2. Sift the cornflour and baking powder. Fold gently through the egg mixture until combined. Place in the tin and level. Bake for 10 – 15 minutes until the mixture springs back when touched.
3. **Filling:** Mix the gelatine and the cold water together well. Leave to sit for 5 minutes.
4. Process the cottage cheese until smooth. Add the cream cheese, yoghurt, sugar or sweetener, lemon rind and juice. Beat until smooth.
5. Melt the gelatine mixture over some boiling water and stir through the cheese mixture.
6. Pour over the base (still in the tin) and refrigerate for 2 – 3 hours until firm.
7. **Topping:** Dissolve the jelly in the boiling water. Leave until nearly set.
8. Place the raspberries, or the cherries that have been halved and the stones removed, on the top of the cheesecake and pour the jelly carefully over the fruit. Refrigerate for 1 hour.

Nutrition Information (per serve) with a cherry and jelly top

Energy: 628 kj (150 cal)   Carbohydrate: 14 g   Fibre: 0.5 g   Total fat: 6.9 g   Saturated fat: 3.8 g   Sodium: 225 mg   GI: Low
GF* Use GF cornflour, baking powder, cottage cheese, cream cheese, yoghurt and jelly.

Macaroon Layered Pavlovas

To make a meringue without huge quantities of sugar is not that easy. The nuts, in this recipe, help make it crisp and yummy. For a change replace the almonds with toasted finely chopped walnuts or hazelnuts.

	2 serves	4 serves	ingredients
Macaroon layer	2 medium	4 medium	egg whites
	3 tablespoons	6 tablespoons	castor sugar
	1/3 cup	2/3 cup	granular Splenda®
	1/2 teaspoon	1 teaspoon	vanilla essence
	1 teaspoon	2 teaspoons	cornflour
	1/2 cup	1 cup	ground almonds
Filling	1 sachet	2 sachets	Weight Watchers® berry flavoured mousse
or	1/2 cup	1 cup	sweetened plain yoghurt
	1 cup	2 cups	fresh berries

1. **Macaroon layer:** Preheat the oven to 120°C (100°C fan). Line a tray with baking paper. Draw 6 (2 serves) or 12 (4 serves), 8 cm diameter circles onto the baking paper.
2. Beat the egg whites until stiff peaks form. While beating add the sugar and Splenda® slowly. Add the essence and cornflour and beat until thick and glossy.
3. Gently fold in the ground almonds.
4. Divide the mixture between the circles and spread to cover the circles.
5. Bake for 1 hour or until the meringue is crisp. When cold place in an airtight container. The meringues will go sticky if left exposed to the air for too long.
6. **Filling:** Make the mousse up according to the instructions on the packet/s.
7. Place a meringue circle onto individual plates, spread with the mousse or yoghurt and then top with some of the berries. Place another meringue circle on top, spread with more mousse or yoghurt and top with some more berries.
8. Place another meringue on top and then decorate the top with the remaining berries.
9. Lightly dust with icing sugar. Serve immediately.

Nutrition Information (per serve) with mousse and fruit filling

Energy: 1601 kj (383 cal)   Carbohydrate: 45 g   Fibre: 1.5 g   Total fat: 17.2 g   Saturated fat: 3 g   Sodium: 133 mg   GI: Low
GF* Use GF cornflour, Weight Watchers® Boysenberry Delight Mousse Mix or yoghurt.

Old Fashioned Spanish Cream

This is such a simple recipe to make, yet with a little effort on presentation, it can look very classy. Milk is a great way of getting calcium in the diet, which helps build healthy bones.

4 serves	ingredients
5 teaspoons	gelatine
2 cups	reduced fat evaporated milk
2 medium	whole eggs
¼ cup	castor sugar[S] or equivalent sweetener[ES]
1 teaspoon	vanilla essence
or 1 teaspoon	instant coffee
4 teaspoons	coffee or Irish Cream liqueur
4	dried figs

1. Mix the gelatine with ¼ cup of the milk. Leave until it swells.
2. Separate the eggs. Beat the yolks, sugar or sweetener and vanilla or coffee together.
3. Heat the remaining milk in a pan until it is nearly boiling.
4. Stir through the egg mixture and continue to cook over a low heat, stirring constantly until the mixture slightly thickens. Remove from the heat.
5. Melt the gelatine mixture over some hot water. Stir it through the custard.
6. Beat the egg whites until thick and foamy. Fold into the custard mixture.
7. Wet some 1 cup moulds, such as tea cups. Pour the mixture into the moulds and refrigerate until set.
8. To remove from the moulds, dip the mould in warm water. Place onto individual plates and drizzle some liqueur around each dessert. Place a halved fig on top and some small pieces around the dessert.

Nutrition Information (per serve) for vanilla flavour

Energy: 1046 kj (250 cal) Carbohydrate: 35 g Fibre: 1.2 g Total fat: 4.7 g Saturated fat: 2 g Sodium: 164 mg GI: Low GF* Use GF evaporated milk.

Jelly Whip

Jelly whip brings back childhood memories. It is a quick dessert to make and it is low in kilojoules (calories). I've added a topping, some berries and put it into individual moulds to make it a bit more exciting.

4 serves	ingredients
1 packet	low calorie berry flavoured jelly crystals
6 tablespoons	hot water
4 teaspoons	no added sugar berry flavoured jam
200 ml	chilled reduced fat evaporated milk
1 cup	fresh berries

1. Dissolve the jelly crystals in the hot water and leave to cool.
2. Wet some 1 cup moulds, such as tea cups. Place a teaspoon of the jam into the base of each cup. Place each cup, individually, in the microwave and cook on high for 10 seconds. Leave to cool.
3. Whip the evaporated milk until thick. Add the jelly and continue to beat until thick. Stir the fruit through quickly, then pour into the moulds. Place in the refrigerator until set.
4. To remove from the mould, dip the mould in warm water.

Nutrition Information (per serve)

Energy: 257 kj (61 cal) Carbohydrate: 8 g Fibre: 0.8 g Total fat: 1.0 g Saturated fat: 0.6 g Sodium: 49 mg GI: Low GF* Use GF evaporated milk, jelly and jam.

Old Fashioned Spanish Cream

Orange Infused Rice Pudding with Dried Fruits

Rice pudding is a winter comfort food for me. This variation is a nice change from the traditional pudding.
To get a creamy rice pudding, using a low fat milk, cook it slowly on the stove top or on low in the microwave.

4 serves	ingredients
4 tablespoons	diced dried apricots
¼ cup	raisins
6 tablespoons	short grain white rice
600 ml	low fat milk
½ teaspoon	vanilla essence
2 teaspoons	grated orange rind
1 medium	cinnamon stick
to taste	white sugar[S] or equivalent sweetener[ES]
200 ml	low fat plain yoghurt
2 tablespoons	toasted sliced almonds

1. Place the apricots, raisins, rice, milk, essence, rind, and cinnamon stick in a microwave proof bowl or a pan.
2. Microwave on low, or cook over a low heat, stirring frequently, until the mixture becomes thick and the rice is soft (30 – 40 minutes).
3. Remove the cinnamon stick. Add the sugar or sweetener to taste.
4. Leave to cool then add the yoghurt and almonds.

Nutrition Information (per serve)

Energy: 1057 kj (253 cal) Carbohydrate: 44 g Fibre: 1.7 g Total fat: 3.5 g Saturated fat: 0.9 g
Sodium: 121 mg GI: Low GF* Use GF yoghurt.

Berry Mousse

I love berries – the colour, texture and taste. From a nutritional perspective they are low in kilojoules (calories),
high in antioxidants and they have a low glycaemic index.

4 serves	ingredients
2 cups	fresh or frozen berries
2 teaspoons	lemon juice
1½ teaspoons	gelatine
250 grams	(8% fat) ricotta cheese
1 cup	low fat plain yoghurt
⅓ cup	castor sugar[S] or equivalent sweetener[ES]
½ cup	fresh berries to garnish

1. Thaw the berries if frozen and remove the juice.
2. Place three quarters of the first measure of berries through a sieve.
3. Combine the lemon juice and gelatine. Leave to swell.
4. In a food processor, process the ricotta, yoghurt and sugar or sweetener together until very smooth.
5. Melt the gelatine mixture over hot water. Add to the ricotta.
6. Divide the mixture into two. Mix the sieved berries through one of the mixtures. Alternate spoonfuls of the plain and berry mixtures into 1 cup parfait glasses and place the remaining berries between the layers.
7. Refrigerate for 2 hours. Garnish with fresh berries.

Nutrition Information (per serve)

Energy: 839 kj (201 cal) Carbohydrate: 22 g Fibre: 1.7 g Total fat: 7.7 g Saturated fat: 4.6 g
Sodium: 107 mg GI: Low GF* Use GF ricotta cheese and yoghurt.

Winter Fruit Compote

Fruit, whether it is fresh, cooked or dried makes a great nutritious base for desserts. This compote is high in fibre and is rather rich – so you only need to eat small amounts. It is delicious served with a reduced fat Greek style yoghurt.

2 serves	4 serves	ingredients
⅓ cup	⅔ cup	dried apricots
3	6	dried dates
5	10	dried prunes
3	6	dried figs
¼ cup	½ cup	chopped dried apple rings
2 tablespoons	¼ cup	dry red wine
¼ cup	½ cup	no added sugar apple juice
1 teaspoon	2 teaspoons	grated orange rind
1 small	1 medium	cinnamon stick
2	4	whole cloves
1 tablespoon	2 tablespoons	toasted slivered almonds

1 | Preheat the oven to 100°C (80°C fan).
2 | Place all the ingredients except the almonds into an ovenproof dish with a lid.
3 | Cook for 1 hour. Stir half way through cooking.
4 | Remove the cinnamon stick and cloves before serving.
5 | Can be served warm or cold, sprinkled with the almonds.

Nutrition Information (per serve)

Energy: 1217 kj (291 cal) Carbohydrate: 60 g Fibre: 6.8 g Total fat: 3.1 g Saturated fat: 0.3 g Sodium: 23 mg GI: Low
GF* No modifications needed.

Hot Chocolate & Berry Souffles

Very few people can resist chocolate. Although this recipe only uses cocoa, it still provides a great chocolate flavour. Cocoa is a way of getting a chocolate flavour with less fat.

2 serves	4 serves	ingredients
½ cup	1 cup	fresh or thawed boysenberries
2 teaspoons	4 teaspoons	no added sugar apple juice concentrate
½ tablespoon	1 tablespoon	cornflour
½ tablespoon	1 tablespoon	cocoa
¾ teaspoon	1½ teaspoons	instant coffee
2 tablespoons	¼ cup	castor sugar
1 tablespoon	2 tablespoons	ground almonds
¼ cup	½ cup	reduced fat evaporated milk
1 teaspoon	2 teaspoons	(70% fat) polyunsaturated margarine
1 medium	2 medium	egg yolk/s
2 medium	4 medium	egg whites

1 Preheat the oven to 180°C (160°C fan). Lightly grease 2 – 4, ¾ cup (185 ml) ramekin dishes.
2 Place the berries in the dishes. Sprinkle 1 teaspoon of the juice into each of the dishes.
3 In a pan combine the cornflour, cocoa, coffee, sugar and almonds.
4 Add a small amount of the milk to form a smooth paste and then stir through the remaining milk. Cook over a low heat until the mixture thickens.
5 Remove from the heat and stir through the margarine until melted.
6 Lightly beat the egg yolk/s and add to the custard mixture.
7 Beat the egg whites until stiff but not dry. Fold into the custard mixture.
8 Pour over the fruit.
9 Bake for 12 – 15 minutes until well risen and browned.
10 Serve immediately. Lightly dust with icing sugar.

Nutrition Information (per serve)

Energy: 865 kj (207 cal) Carbohydrate: 26 g Fibre: 1.3 g Total fat: 7.5 g Saturated fat: 1.8 g Sodium: 125 mg GI: Medium
GF* Use GF cornflour, cocoa and evaporated milk.

Spiced Bread & Butter Puddings

This bread pudding looks great made into small individual loaves. Individual loaf tins look like muffin tins but are rectangular rather than being round. They are available from most kitchen shops and some supermarkets.

2 serves	4 serves	ingredients
3 slices	6 slices	spicy fruit bread
3	6	dried apricots
1 tablespoon	2 tablespoons	dried currants
1 medium	2 medium	whole egg/s
¼ cup	½ cup	low fat milk
¼ cup	½ cup	reduced fat evaporated milk
½ teaspoon	1 teaspoon	vanilla essence
1 tablespoon	2 tablespoons	castor sugar
1 tablespoon	2 tablespoons	flaked almonds
sprinkle	sprinkle	cinnamon

1. Preheat the oven to 180°C (160°C fan). Line the bases and sides of 2 – 4, (½ cup) mini loaf tins with baking paper. Muffin tins or ramekins can be used instead – the bread would have to be cut differently to fit these shapes.
2. Remove the crusts from the bread. Chop 2 slices (2 serves) or 4 slices (4 serves) of the bread into halves. Chop the apricots into small cubes.
3. In each tin, place a layer of bread, followed by a layer of apricots and currants. Add another layer of bread and of apricots and currants.
4. Chop the remaining bread into quarters. Cut each quarter into half, diagonally to form triangles.
5. Place four bread triangles, overlapping each other, on top of the pudding. Sprinkle over the remaining dried fruit.
6. Lightly beat the egg/s, milks, essence and sugar.
7. Pour over the bread and leave to stand for 10 minutes.
8. Sprinkle over the almonds and cinnamon. Bake for 20 – 25 minutes or until cooked and browned.

Nutrition Information (per serve)

Energy: 1055 kj (252 cal) Carbohydrate: 37 g Fibre: 2.3 g Total fat: 6.1 g Saturated fat: 1.6 g Sodium: 248 mg GI: Low
GF* Use GF evaporated milk and Venerdi's™ GF fruit bread.

Poached Pears with a Fruit & Nut Stuffing

Pears may taste sweet, but despite this, they have a low glycaemic index. This fig and hazelnut stuffing is interesting and looks great when the pears are cut in half, to be served.

2 serves	4 serves	ingredients
2 medium	4 medium	eating pears
3	6	dried figs
2 tablespoons	4 tablespoons	toasted hazelnuts
¼ teaspoon	½ teaspoon	ground cinnamon
⅓ cup	⅔ cup	dry red wine
1 tablespoon	2 tablespoons	apple juice concentrate
⅓ cup	⅔ cup	cold water
1 strip	2 strips	orange rind
1 small	1 medium	cinnamon stick
1	2	whole clove/s

1. Preheat the oven to 160°C (140°C fan).
2. Peel the pears. Scoop out the cores from the bottom of the pears, leaving the stem intact.
3. In a food processor, process the figs, nuts and cinnamon until finely ground. Stuff the pears tightly with this mixture. Place upright in an ovenproof dish.
4. Combine the wine, juice, water, rind, cinnamon stick and clove/s together. Pour the liquid over the pears.
5. Cover and bake for 45 – 60 minutes until the pears are cooked but still firm. Every 10 minutes spoon the liquid over the pears.
6. Remove from the oven and pour the liquid into a pan. Keep the pears warm.
7. Cook the liquid over a medium heat until it becomes a thick syrup. Remove the cinnamon stick and cloves.
8. Chop the pears in half and serve on a plate overlapping each other. Pour the syrup around the pears and serve immediately.

Nutrition Information (per serve)

Energy: 959 kj (229 cal) Carbohydrate: 32 g Fibre: 5.6 g Total fat: 5.9 g Saturated fat: 0.6 g Sodium: 19 mg GI: Low
GF* No modifications needed.

Fruit Shortcake Crumble

Everyone who has tasted this shortcake has always raved about it – a good sign that it tastes great.
The recipe has 2 filling options, equally as good as each other.

	8 – 12 serves	ingredients	8 – 12 serves	ingredients
Pastry	4½ tablespoons	(70% fat) polyunsaturated margarine		Rhubarb and Pear or Apple:
			400 grams	fresh rhubarb
	1½ tablespoons	icing sugar	5 medium	eating pears or apples
	1 tablespoon	custard powder	½ cup	concentrated apple juice
	1 cup & 2T	plain flour	½ teaspoon	ground ginger
	1 teaspoon	baking powder	¼ teaspoon	ground cloves
	1½ tablespoons	ground almonds	½ cup	white sugar^S or equivalent
	¼ cup & 2T	low fat milk		sweetener^ES
Fillings		Apple and Boysenberry:		Topping
	1½ cups	frozen boysenberries	½ cup	rolled oats
	400 grams	canned apple, in natural juice	2 tablespoons	low fat milk
	½ cup	castor sugar^S or equivalent	4 dessertspoons	hazelnuts or slivered almonds
		sweetener^ES	½ teaspoon	ground cinnamon

1. **Pastry:** In a food processor or mixer place the margarine, icing sugar, custard powder, flour, baking powder and almonds. Mix until the mixture resembles fine breadcrumbs.
2. Add the milk until the mixture is soft and combined. Refrigerate for 30 minutes.
3. **Filling (Apple and Boysenberry):** Leave the boysenberries to thaw. Remove the juice.
   Gently combine the boysenberries with the apple and sugar or sweetener.
4. **Filling (Rhubarb and Pear or Apple):** Chop the rhubarb into small pieces. Leaving the skins on, core the pears or apples and chop into small pieces. Place in a pan with the juice, ginger and cloves. Simmer until the fruit is soft. Add the sugar or sweetener and leave to cool.
5. **Assembly:** Preheat the oven to 180°C (160°C fan). Lightly grease a 24 cm round flan tin.
6. Roll out three quarters of the pastry to fit the base and sides of the tin. Spread over the fruit.
7. **Topping:** Combine the remaining pastry with the oats and milk. Dot over the fruit. Sprinkle over the nuts and cinnamon. Bake for 35 minutes or until cooked. Serve warm or cold, lightly dusted with icing sugar.

Nutrition Information (per serve) for the pear and rhubarb filling, based on serving 12
Energy: 690 kj (165 cal) Carbohydrate: 25 g Fibre: 2.7 g Total fat: 6.0 g Saturated fat: 1.1 g Sodium: 60 mg GI: Low

Fruit & Custard Cake

This is a delicious cake layered with custard and fruit. You could substitute the pear and rhubarb with apple and boysenberries. It is best eaten warm from the oven or reheated in the microwave.

10 serves	ingredients	10 serves	ingredients
1 cup	low fat milk	150 grams	fresh rhubarb
2 tablespoons	custard powder	1 medium	eating pear
½ teaspoon	vanilla essence	75 grams	reduced fat (<56% fat)
1 tablespoon	white sugar[S] or equivalent sweetener[ES]		polyunsaturated margarine
		¼ cup	castor sugar
1 cup	plain flour	½ cup	granular Splenda[®ES] or castor sugar[S]
4 teaspoons	baking powder		
2 tablespoons	custard powder	1 cup	buttermilk
½ cup	oat bran	1 medium	egg yolk
½ cup	ground almonds	3 medium	egg whites

1. Preheat the oven to 170°C (150°C fan). Line the base of a 20 cm round cake tin with baking paper and lightly grease the sides.
2. Mix to a smooth paste, ¼ cup of the low fat milk with the first measure of the custard powder.
3. Bring the remaining low fat milk and essence to the boil. Add the custard paste and the first measure of sugar or sweetener and stir until thickened. Place some heat resistant cling film on the surface of the custard to stop a skin forming. Leave to cool.
4. Sift the flour, baking powder and the second measure of the custard powder. Add the oat bran and almonds.
5. Slice the rhubarb into small pieces. Leaving the skin on the pear, chop into quarters and core. Slice into long thin slivers.
6. Beat the margarine and the second measure of sugar and the Splenda® or the third measure of sugar until creamy. Add the yolk to the creamed mixture.
7. Gently fold through the dry ingredients and the buttermilk. Beat the egg whites until thick and foamy. Gently fold into the mixture. Place half of the mixture into the tin and level.
8. Spread the custard over the cake, leaving a 2 cm border around the edges. Layer over, half of the fruit. Spread over the remaining cake mixture and then place the remaining fruit decoratively on the top.
9. Bake for 60 – 75 minutes or until cooked. Leave in the tin for 10 minutes then place on a cooling rack to cool.
10. Refrigerate the cake until serving if it isn't eaten warm from the oven. To serve, lightly dust with icing sugar.

Nutrition Information (per serve)

Energy: 867 kj (207 cal) Carbohydrate: 28 g Fibre: 1.7 g Total fat: 7.9 g Saturated fat: 1.1 g Sodium: 268 mg GI: Medium

NOSH: desserts

baking

Snacking can result in eating too many kilojoules and too much fat, sugar and salt – if you snack too often and on the wrong foods. Snack foods are not treat foods. Snacks are those foods that can be eaten on a regular basis (lower fat, sugar and kilojoules and higher fibre) and treats are foods that are eaten occasionally (higher fat, sugar and kilojoules and lower fibre).

Muffins are not always healthy. Quite often they are mini versions of cakes – with lots of butter and sugar, and little fibre, and the portion sizes are far too big. NOSH muffins are flavoursome, healthy and moist which means that you definitely don't need to butter them.

For most people, biscuits, slices and cakes should be treated as occasional foods. Make them when you have visitors – that way the kilojoules are shared amongst a number of waist lines!

NOSH baking recipes are best made and eaten fresh. However, the muffins, scones and loaves freeze well. Reheat them in a microwave – they taste like they have come straight out of the oven!

Pear, Blue Cheese & Walnut Muffins

The cheese flavour is subtle in these muffins – even people who dislike blue cheese enjoyed them. The oats and oat bran add some soluble fibre helping to lower the glyceamic index.

	6 serves	12 serves	ingredients
	¾ cup	1 ½ cups	plain flour
	2 teaspoons	4 teaspoons	baking powder
	¼ cup	½ cup	oat bran
	¼ cup	½ cup	wholegrain oats
	2 tablespoons	¼ cup	chopped walnuts
	1 (150 grams)	2 (300 grams)	eating pear/s
	25 grams	50 grams	blue vein cheese
	1 small	2 small	whole egg/s
	½ cup	1 cup	low fat milk
	1 tablespoon	2 tablespoons	vegetable oil
Topping	½ medium	1 medium	eating pear
(optional)	6 squares	12 squares	blue cheese
	6	12	walnut halves

1. Preheat the oven to 200°C (180°C fan). Lightly grease 6 – 12 (½ cup) muffin tins.
2. Sift the flour and baking powder together. Add the oat bran, oats and the first measure of walnuts.
3. Leaving the skin on, core and chop the first measure of pear/s into small chunks.
4. Slice the first measure of cheese finely. Beat the egg/s, milk and oil together.
5. Combine all the ingredients together and stir gently until just combined. Do not over mix.
6. Spoon into the muffin tins.
7. Slice the remaining pear into quarters and then into thin slices. Top the muffins with a square of the cheese, a slice of pear and a walnut half.
8. Bake for 13 – 15 minutes or until cooked and browned.
9. Leave to sit in the tins for 5 minutes before turning out onto a cooling rack.
10. Best eaten fresh (1 – 2 days) or frozen and then reheated in the microwave.

Nutrition Information (per serve)

Energy: 816 kj (195 cal) Carbohydrate: 22 g Fibre: 2.4 g Total fat: 8.8 g Saturated fat: 2.0 g Sodium: 216 mg GI: Medium

Mediterranean Muffins (left) and Pear, Blue Cheese and Walnut Muffins pg 125 (right)

Mediterranean Muffins

Savoury muffins are often full of cheese and are therefore high in fat. These muffins are full of flavour without all the fat. Using oil in baked products, helps make them moist.

6 serves	12 serves	ingredients
¾ cup	1½ cups	plain flour
2 teaspoons	4 teaspoons	baking powder
½ cup	1 cup	oat bran
25 grams	50 grams	feta cheese
1 small	2 small	whole egg/s
¾ cup	1½ cups	low fat milk
1 tablespoon	2 tablespoons	vegetable oil
1 tablespoon	2 tablespoons	diced green pepper
1 tablespoon	2 tablespoons	diced red pepper or sun dried tomatoes
1 tablespoon	2 tablespoons	diced red onion
1 tablespoon	2 tablespoons	basil, olive or tomato pesto
2 teaspoons	4 teaspoons	pine nuts
Topping 3	6	black olives (optional)

1   Preheat the oven to 200°C (180°C fan). Lightly grease 6 – 12 (½ cup) muffin tins.
2   Sift the flour and baking powder together. Add the oat bran.
3   Chop the feta cheese into small cubes. Beat the egg/s, milk and oil together.
4   Combine all the ingredients, except the olives, and stir gently until just combined. Do not over mix.
5   Spoon into the muffin tins. Remove the stones from the olives and chop each olive in half. Place a halved olive on the top of each muffin.
6   Bake for 13 – 15 minutes or until cooked and browned.
7   Leave to sit in the tins for 5 minutes before turning out onto a cooling rack.
8   Best eaten fresh (1 – 2 days) or frozen and then reheated in the microwave.

Nutrition Information (per serve)
Energy: 691 kj (165 cal)   Carbohydrate: 20 g   Fibre: 1.9 g   Total fat: 6.9 g   Saturated fat: 1.5 g   Sodium: 259 mg   GI: Medium

Blueberry Spice Muffins

Muffins are not always healthy. Quite often they are mini versions of cakes – with lots of butter and sugar, and little fibre in them. The portion sizes, are sometimes, far too big.

6 serves	12 serves	ingredients
¾ cup	1½ cups	plain flour
2 teaspoons	4 teaspoons	baking powder
½ teaspoon	1 teaspoon	ground allspice
⅓ cup	⅔ cup	oat bran
1 tablespoon	2 tablespoons	lightly packed brown sugar
1 medium	2 medium	whole egg/s
½ cup	1 cup	low fat milk
1 tablespoon	2 tablespoons	vegetable oil
1 large (150 grams)	2 large (300 grams)	banana/s
½ cup	1 cup	fresh or frozen blueberries
Topping 18	36	fresh or frozen blueberries

1. Preheat the oven to 190°C (170°C fan). Lightly grease 6 – 12 (½ cup) muffin tins.
2. Sift the flour, baking powder and spice together. Add the oat bran and sugar.
3. Lightly beat the egg/s with the milk. Add the oil.
4. Mash the banana.
5. Add the egg mixture, banana and the first measure of blueberries to the dry ingredients. Stir gently until just combined. Do not over mix.
6. Spoon into the muffin tins and place 3 blueberries on the top of each muffin.
7. Bake for 15 – 20 minutes or until the muffins are cooked and browned.
8. Leave to sit in the tins for 5 minutes before turning out onto a cooling rack.
9. Best eaten fresh (1 – 2 days) or frozen and then reheated in the microwave.

Nutrition Information (per serve)

Energy: 659 kj (158 cal) Carbohydrate: 26 g Fibre: 2.1 g Total fat: 4 g Saturated fat: 0.6 g Sodium: 161 mg GI: Medium

Muffins from front to back: Blueberry Spice Muffins, Pear, Blue Cheese and Walnut Muffins pg 125, Apple Streusel Muffins pg 130 and Mediterranean Muffins pg 127

Apple Streusel Muffins

Adding fruit to baked products, such as muffins, increases their nutritional value and makes them moist. It also reduces the amount of extra sugar needed, therefore reducing the overall kilojoule value of the baked product.

6 serves	12 serves	ingredients
¾ cup	1½ cups	plain flour
2 teaspoons	4 teaspoons	baking powder
1 teaspoon	2 teaspoons	ground cinnamon
1 teaspoon	2 teaspoons	ground ginger
1 teaspoon	2 teaspoons	ground mixed spice
pinch	¼ teaspoon	ground cloves
¼ cup	½ cup	oat bran
¼ cup	½ cup	rolled oats
3 tablespoons	6 tablespoons	flaked almonds
1 medium	2 medium	whole egg/s
¾ cup	1½ cups	low fat milk
1 tablespoon	2 tablespoons	vegetable oil
2 tablespoons	4 tablespoons	golden syrup
2 tablespoons	4 tablespoons	castor sugar[S] or equivalent sweetener[ES]
½ x 400 gram can	1 x 400 gram can	apples, in natural juice

Topping (optional)

6 serves	12 serves	ingredients
1 medium	2 medium	eating apple/s
sprinkle	sprinkle	ground cinnamon

1. Preheat the oven to 180°C (160°C fan). Lightly grease 6 – 12 (½ cup) muffin tins.
2. Sift the flour, baking powder, first measure of cinnamon, ginger, mixed spice and cloves. Add the oat bran, oats and almonds.
3. Lightly beat the egg/s with the milk and oil. Add the syrup, castor sugar or sweetener and canned apple. Stir gently through the dry ingredients until just combined. Do not over mix.
4. Spoon into the muffin tins.
5. Chop the eating apple/s into thin rounds and remove the seeds. Discard the outer slices. Place one slice on top of each muffin then sprinkle with the second measure of cinnamon.
6. Bake for 12 – 18 minutes or until cooked and browned.
7. Leave to sit in the tins for 5 minutes before turning out onto a cooling rack.
8. Best eaten fresh (1 – 2 days) or frozen and then reheated in the microwave.

Nutrition Information (per serve)

Energy: 773 kj (185 cal) Carbohydrate: 27 g Fibre: 2.9 g Total fat: 6.2 g Saturated fat: 0.8 g Sodium: 175 mg GI: Medium

Pizza Pinwheels

Baked products often only use plain (white) flour which has the fibre removed. Up to half of the plain flour can be substituted with wholemeal flour, and a bit less with oat bran, without making the product too heavy and dry. Additional liquid is needed to compensate for the extra fibre.

	5 serves	10 serves	ingredients
Filling	½ medium	1 medium	red onion
	⅓ cup	⅔ cup	diced lean bacon
	¼ cup	½ cup	diced green pepper
	50 grams	100 grams	grated tasty cheese
	3 tablespoons	6 tablespoons	low fat cottage cheese
	½ teaspoon	1 teaspoon	mixed dried herbs
Scone mixture	½ cup & 2T	1 ¼ cups	plain flour
	2 teaspoons	4 teaspoons	baking powder
	½ tablespoon	1 tablespoon	low fat milk powder
	pinch	pinch	iodised salt
	¼ cup & 2T	¾ cup	oat bran
	1 tablespoon	2 tablespoons	(70% fat) polyunsaturated margarine
	¼ – ½ cup	½ – 1 cup	low fat milk
	2½ tablespoons	5 tablespoons	no added salt tomato paste

1. **Filling:** Finely dice the onion. Place the onion, bacon and green pepper in a non–stick frying pan and fry until softened. Leave to cool. Add the tasty cheese, cottage cheese and herbs.
2. **Scone mixture:** Preheat the oven to 200°C (180°C fan). Lightly grease an oven tray.
3. Sift the flour, baking powder, milk powder and salt. Add the oat bran.
4. Rub the margarine into the dry ingredients until the mixture resembles fine crumbs. Add the milk to form a soft dough.
5. **Assembling:** Roll the dough out to form a 30 x 30 cm square (5 scones) or a 30 x 60 cm rectangle (10 scones).
6. Spread the tomato paste over the dough and scatter over the filling.
7. Roll up and slice into 3 cm sized slices. Place on the oven tray and bake for 15 – 20 minutes or until cooked and browned.
8. Best eaten fresh (1 – 2 days) or frozen and then reheated in the microwave.

Nutrition Information (per serve)
Energy: 751 kj (180 cal) Carbohydrate: 20 g Fibre: 2.0 g Total fat: 6.8 g Saturated fat: 3.0 g Sodium: 425 mg GI: Medium

Ham & Pineapple Mini Loaves

My taste testers told me that these are the nicest scones that they have ever tasted! Parmesan cheese is a great substitute for cheddar cheese as it is highly flavoured and therefore you only need small amounts to get maximum flavour.

4 serves	8 serves	ingredients
¼ cup & 2T	¾ cup	plain flour
2½ teaspoons	5 teaspoons	baking powder
¼ cup & 2T	¾ cup	wholemeal flour
1 slice	2 slices	lean ham
½ small	1 small	red onion
¼ cup	½ cup	crushed pineapple, in natural juice
1 tablespoon	2 tablespoons	whole seed mustard
½ tablespoon	1 tablespoon	vegetable oil
¼ cup	½ cup	low fat cottage cheese
½ tablespoon	1 tablespoon	grated parmesan cheese
1 teaspoon	2 teaspoons	French onion soup powder
⅛ cup	¼ cup	low fat milk

Topping

4 serves	8 serves	ingredients
1 teaspoon	2 teaspoons	whole seed mustard
2 tablespoons	¼ cup	grated Edam cheese
½ tablespoon	1 tablespoon	pumpkin seeds

1. Preheat the oven to 200°C (180°C fan). Lightly grease 4 – 8 (½ cup) mini loaf tins.
2. Sift the plain flour and baking powder. Add the wholemeal flour.
3. Dice the ham and onion into small cubes. Fry until softened. Leave to cool.
4. Drain the pineapple.
5. Add the ham mixture, pineapple, first measure of whole seed mustard, oil, cottage cheese, parmesan cheese, soup powder and milk to the dry ingredients to form a soft sticky dough.
6. Divide the mixture into 4 – 8 pieces and shape to fit the loaf tins. Spread the top with the second measure of mustard then sprinkle over the Edam cheese and pumpkin seeds.
7. Bake for 15 minutes then reduce the oven to 180°C (160°C fan) and cook for another 10 minutes or until cooked.
8. Best eaten fresh (1 – 2 days) or frozen and then reheated in the microwave.

Nutrition Information (per serve)

Energy: 668 kj (160 cal) Carbohydrate: 21 g Fibre: 2.1 g Total fat: 4.8 g Saturated fat: 1.3 g Sodium: 413 mg GI: Medium

Plain or Dried Fruit Scones

The amount of baking powder, in this recipe, is not a mistake. When wholemeal flour or bran are added to baked products, additional baking powder is needed to make them lighter.

6 serves	12 serves	ingredients
1 ¼ cups	2 ½ cups	plain flour
4 teaspoons	8 teaspoons	baking powder
1 tablespoon	2 tablespoons	low fat milk powder
pinch	pinch	iodised salt
¾ cup	1 ½ cups	oat bran
1 teaspoon	2 teaspoons	castor sugar
2 tablespoons	¼ cup	(70% fat) polyunsaturated margarine
about ¾ cup	about 1 ½ cups	low fat milk
Flavour options		Date and Lemon:
½ cup	1 cup	chopped dried dates
1 teaspoon	2 teaspoons	grated lemon rind
		Sultana and Orange:
½ cup	1 cup	sultanas
1 teaspoon	2 teaspoons	grated orange rind

1 Preheat the oven to 210°C (190°C fan). Lightly grease an oven tray.
2 Sift the flour, baking powder, milk powder and salt. Add the oat bran and sugar.
3 Rub in the margarine until the mixture resembles fine crumbs.
4 For the fruit scones, add the dates and lemon rind or the sultanas and orange rind.
5 Add the milk to form a soft dough.
6 Turn onto a floured board and roll out to a 2 cm thickness. Chop into 6 –12, 7cm squares or rounds. Place on the oven tray and bake for 12 – 15 minutes until cooked.
7 Place on a cooling rack. For crusty scones leave uncovered and for soft scones wrap in a tea towel.
8 Best eaten fresh (1 – 2 days) or frozen and then reheated in the microwave.

Nutrition Information (per serve) for a plain scone
Energy: 818 kj (196 cal) Carbohydrate: 31 g Fibre: 2.7 g Total fat: 5.5 g Saturated fat: 1.0 g Sodium: 365 mg GI: Medium

Plain Scone

Mixed Fruit Scrolls

Margarine is a suitable substitute for butter in cooking. Standard margarines contain nearly as much fat as butter, but they are much lower in saturated fats. Do not use light or fat reduced margarines unless the recipe specifies. These margarines have a high water content and will not always work in recipes.

	5 serves	10 serves	ingredients
Filling mixture	½ medium	1 medium	eating apple
	¼ cup	½ cup	dried apricots
	6	12	dried dates
	¼ cup	½ cup	sultanas
	½ teaspoon	1 teaspoon	ground mixed spice
	½ cup	1 cup	no added sugar orange juice
	1 tablespoon	2 tablespoons	cold water
Scone mixture	½ cup & 2T	1 ¼ cups	plain flour
	2 teaspoons	4 teaspoons	baking powder
	½ tablespoon	1 tablespoon	low fat milk powder
	pinch	pinch	iodised salt
	¼ cup & 2T	¾ cup	oat bran
	1 tablespoon	2 tablespoons	(70% fat) polyunsaturated margarine
	¼ – ½ cup	½ – 1 cup	low fat milk
	2 tablespoons	¼ cup	sliced almonds

1   **Filling mixture:** Keeping the skin on the apple, core and chop into small chunks. Dice the apricots and dates into small cubes.
2   Place the apple, apricots, dates, sultanas, mixed spice, juice and water into a pan. Simmer for 5 minutes or until the fruit is soft. Leave to cool.
3   **Scone mixture:** Preheat the oven to 200°C (180°C fan). Lightly grease an oven tray.
4   Sift the flour, baking powder, milk powder and salt. Add the oat bran.
5   Rub the margarine into the dry ingredients until the mixture resembles fine crumbs. Add the milk to form a soft dough.
6   Roll the dough out to form a 30 x 30 cm square (5 scones) or a 30 x 60 cm rectangle (10 scones).
7   **Assembling:** Spread the fruit mixture then the nuts over the dough and roll up. Slice into 3 cm sized slices. Place on the oven tray and bake for 15 minutes or until cooked.
8   Best eaten fresh (1 – 2 days) or frozen and then reheated in the microwave.

Nutrition Information (per serve)
Energy: 941 kj (225 cal)   Carbohydrate: 38 g   Fibre: 3.4 g   Total fat: 5.8 g   Saturated fat: 0.9 g   Sodium: 227 mg   GI: Medium

Fruit Salad Loaf

This loaf has a really nice flavour. If you are not fond of a banana flavour, in baking, don't be put off this recipe – the flavour is very subtle.

12 serves	ingredients
½ cup	dried apricots
1 teaspoon	grated orange rind
1 teaspoon	grated lemon rind
¼ cup	orange juice
¼ cup	lemon juice
75 grams	reduced fat (<56% fat) polyunsaturated margarine
¼ cup	lightly packed brown sugar
2 tablespoons	castor sugar[S] or granular Splenda® [ES]
¾ cup	plain flour
1 tablespoon	baking powder
¾ cup	wholemeal flour
½ cup	oat bran
1 medium	eating apple
⅓ cup	mashed banana
1 medium	whole egg
Topping 2 tablespoons	flaked almonds

1. Preheat the oven to 180°C (160°C fan). Line a loaf tin (13 x 23 cm) with baking paper.
2. Slice the apricots into small cubes. Place in a pan with the orange and lemon rinds and juices, margarine, brown sugar and castor sugar or Splenda®. Bring to the boil then remove from the heat and cool.
3. Sift the plain flour and baking powder. Add the wholemeal flour and oat bran.
4. Leaving the skin on the apple, core then grate. Mix the banana with the egg.
5. Combine all the ingredients together, except the almonds and gently combine. Do not over mix.
6. Place in the loaf tin. Sprinkle with the almonds.
7. Bake for 40 – 45 minutes or until cooked. Leave in the tin for 5 minutes then place on a cooling rack to cool.
8. Best eaten fresh (1 – 2 days) or frozen and then reheated in the microwave.

Nutrition Information (per serve)

Energy: 616 kj (147 cal) Carbohydrate: 23 g Fibre: 2.5 g Total fat: 4.6 g Saturated fat: 0.7 g Sodium: 149 mg GI: Medium

Banana & Prune Loaf

Nuts and seeds add a different texture in baking. They are high in fat (and kilojoules), but the fat that is predominant in them is beneficial for heart health.

15 serves	ingredients
¾ cup	dried prunes
1 teaspoon	baking soda
¾ cup	boiling water
1 cup	plain flour
1 tablespoon	baking powder
1 cup	wholemeal flour
¼ cup	lightly packed brown sugar
¼ cup	castor sugar^S or equivalent sweetener^{ES}
⅓ cup	chopped walnuts
2 medium	whole eggs
½ cup	low fat milk
2 (250 grams)	bananas
2 tablespoons	vegetable oil

1   Preheat the oven to 180°C (160°C fan). Line a loaf tin (13 x 23 cm) with baking paper.
2   Chop the prunes into small pieces and place in a bowl. Sprinkle over the baking soda and water. Leave for 10 minutes.
3   Sift the plain flour and baking powder. Add the wholemeal flour, brown sugar, castor sugar or sweetener and nuts.
4   Beat the eggs with the milk.
5   Mash the bananas and add the oil.
6   Combine all the ingredients together gently. Do not over mix.
7   Place in the loaf tin and bake for 45 – 50 minutes or until cooked. Leave in the tin for 5 minutes then place on a cooling rack to cool.
8   Best eaten fresh (1 – 2 days) or frozen and then reheated in the microwave.

Nutrition Information (per serve)
Energy: 617 kj (148 cal)   Carbohydrate: 23 g   Fibre: 2.0 g   Total fat: 4.6 g   Saturated fat: 0.6 g   Sodium: 140 mg   GI: Medium

Multigrain Bread

The smell of bread cooking is irresistible. This is a great recipe – it has lots of fibre in it and yet it is very light and fluffy. Adding wholegrains to bread will decrease the glycaemic index.

23 serves	ingredients
1 cup	plain flour
1 ½ cups	wholemeal flour
½ cup	gluten flour
½ cup	oat bran
1 cup	Bin Inn's mixed grains bread base
2 tablespoons	sunflower seeds
1 teaspoon	iodised salt
2 tablespoons	Surebake® yeast
1 tablespoon	lightly packed brown sugar
1 ½ cups	lukewarm water
1 tablespoon	olive oil
light spray	oil
sprinkle	sesame seeds
sprinkle	rolled oats

1. Combine the flours, oat bran, grains, seeds, salt, yeast and sugar.
2. Add the water and oil. If the mixture is too soft add more wholemeal flour. Knead for 10 minutes until smooth and elastic. Place in a greased large bowl. Cover with cling film and stand in a warm place until doubled in size (1 – 1½ hours). Punch down the dough. Knead for 10 minutes.
3. Grease a loaf tin (13 cm x 23 cm). Shape the dough to fit the tin. Spray with oil then sprinkle over some sesame seeds and rolled oats.
4. Cover and stand in a warm place for about 30 minutes or until well risen.
5. Preheat the oven to 200°C (180°C fan).
6. Cook for 45 minutes or until cooked (should sound hollow when the top is tapped). Leave in the tin for 10 minutes then place on a cooling rack to cool.
7. Best eaten fresh (1 – 2 days) or frozen and then thawed and toasted.

Nutrition Information (per serve)

Energy: 424 kj (101 cal) Carbohydrate: 19 g Fibre: 2.4 g Total fat: 1.6 g Saturated fat: 0.3 g Sodium: 104 mg GI: Medium

Chelsea Buns pg 143 (left) and Multigrain Bread (right)

Chelsea Buns

Chelsea Buns or Fruit Bread

Gluten flour, which is available from supermarkets, helps produce a better textured dough.

12 – 23 serves	ingredients	12 – 23 serves	ingredients
2 cups	plain high grade flour	2 tablespoons	olive oil
½ cup	wholemeal flour	10	dried apricots
3 tablespoons	gluten flour	1 medium	whole egg
½ cup	oat bran	¼ cup	low fat milk
1 tablespoon	linseed	1 medium	whole egg
1 teaspoon	iodised salt	2 teaspoons	grated orange rind
2 tablespoons	lightly packed brown sugar	2 teaspoons	ground cinnamon
2 tablespoons	Surebake® yeast	2 teaspoons	mixed spice
2 tablespoons	lukewarm water	¼ cup	chopped walnuts
1 cup	warm low fat milk	½ cup	dried currants

1   **Basic Dough:** Combine the flours, oat bran, linseed, salt, sugar and yeast.
2   Add the water, first measure of milk and oil. Knead for 10 minutes or until smooth and elastic.
3   Place in a lightly greased large bowl. Cover with cling film and stand in a warm place until doubled in size (1 – 1½ hours). Meanwhile, finely slice the apricots into small pieces.
4   Make the glaze by beating the first egg and remaining milk together. Refrigerate until required.
5   **Chelsea Buns:** Grease two 20 cm round cake tins, or line 12 (½ cup) muffin tins with baking paper. Punch down the dough. Add the second egg, rind and half of the spices. Knead for 10 minutes or until smooth and elastic.
6   Roll out to form a rectangle 25 cm by 50 cm. Spread with ½ cup of a no added sugar berry flavoured jam.
7   Sprinkle over the dried apricots, remaining spices, walnuts and currants. Roll up starting from the long side. Slice into 12 pieces. Place 6 buns, evenly spaced, into each round cake tin, or one bun into each muffin tin. Cover and leave in a warm place to double in size. Brush over the glaze. Preheat the oven to 200°C (180°C fan) and bake for 10 minutes, then at 180°C (160°C fan) for 5 – 15 minutes or until cooked.
8   **Fruit Bread:** Punch down the dough. Add the apricots and the second egg, rind, spices, walnuts and currants. Knead for 10 minutes or until smooth and elastic.
9   Lightly grease a loaf tin (13 x 23 cm). Shape the dough to fit the tin, cover and leave to rise for 30 minutes or until doubled in size. Brush over the glaze. Preheat the oven to 200°C (180°C fan) and bake for 40 minutes or until cooked. Cut into 23 slices.

Nutrition Information (per serve) for Chelsea Buns
Energy: 829 kj (198 cal)   Carbohydrate: 31 g   Fibre: 2.8 g   Total fat: 5.6 g   Saturated fat: 1.0 g   Sodium: 219 mg   GI: Medium

Blueberry Yoghurt Pikelets

The blueberries in this recipe can be substituted with other berries such as raspberries, boysenberries and blackberries. Berries, particularly frozen ones, bleed so it is best to add them at the end.

12 serves	ingredients
1 medium	whole egg
½ cup	low fat milk
1 tablespoon	castor sugar
1 teaspoon	vegetable oil
¼ cup	low fat berry flavoured yoghurt
¼ cup	rolled oats
½ cup	plain flour
1 teaspoon	baking powder
½ teaspoon	baking soda
½ cup	fresh or frozen blueberries

1. Beat the egg with the milk. Stir through the sugar, oil, yoghurt and oats. Cover and refrigerate for 30 minutes.
2. Sift the flour, baking powder and baking soda. Add to the egg mixture and mix well.
3. Heat a non–stick frying pan over a low heat. Place 2 tablespoonfuls of the mixture in the pan to make each pikelet. Sprinkle over some blueberries. When the bubbles appear turn the pikelets over. Remove from the pan when cooked.
4. Wrap in a tea towel on a cooling rack. They are best eaten on the day that they are made or frozen and reheated in the microwave.

Nutrition Information (per serve)

Energy: 201 kj (48 cal)   Carbohydrate: 8 g   Fibre: 0.4 g   Total fat: 1.1 g   Saturated fat: 0.2 g   Sodium: 100 mg   GI: Medium

Fruit Biscuits

It is never easy to make biscuits without a large amount of fat and sugar. The fat helps bind the biscuits and adds flavour. Some sugar is needed to make biscuits crisp and to brown them.

12 serves	24 serves	ingredients
3 tablespoons	⅓ cup	sultanas
3 tablespoons	⅓ cup	dried currants
3 tablespoons	⅓ cup	dried apricots
1 tablespoon	2 tablespoons	no added sugar orange juice
½ cup	1 cup	plain flour
½ teaspoon	1 teaspoon	baking powder
¼ cup	½ cup	oat bran
1½ tablespoons	3 tablespoons	low fat milk powder
¼ teaspoon	½ teaspoon	ground mixed spice
¼ teaspoon	½ teaspoon	ground cinnamon
50 grams	100 grams	(70% fat) polyunsaturated margarine
1½ tablespoons	3 tablespoons	honey
¼ cup	½ cup	castor sugar[S] or granular Splenda[®ES]
¼ teaspoon	½ teaspoon	almond essence (optional)

1. Preheat the oven to 150°C (130°C fan). Lightly grease 1 – 2 oven trays.
2. In a food processor, process the sultanas, currants, apricots with the juice until finely minced.
3. Combine the flour, baking powder, oat bran, milk powder, mixed spice and cinnamon.
4. Beat the margarine with the honey, sugar or Splenda® and essence until creamy.
5. Add the processed fruit and the dry ingredients. Mix to form a soft dough.
6. Roll into 12 balls (12 serves) or 24 balls (24 serves). Place on the oven tray/s. Place a 6 cm round biscuit cutter over a biscuit and flatten to fit this. Remove the cutter and repeat with the remaining biscuits.
7. Bake for 20 – 25 minutes or until cooked and browned. Leave to sit for 5 minutes before placing on a cooling rack. When cold, place in an airtight container. Will keep 2 weeks.

Nutrition Information (per serve)

Energy: 365 kj (87 cal) Carbohydrate: 12 g Fibre: 0.8 g Total fat: 3.6 g Saturated fat: 0.6 g Sodium: 58 mg GI: Low

Coffee & Hazelnut Biscotti

Biscotti is usually lower in fat than most biscuits. The double cooking helps it to become crisp without the need for a lot of sugar. Coffee and hazelnut are perfect partners for flavour!

25 serves	ingredients
1 cup	plain flour
½ teaspoon	baking powder
1 tablespoon	instant coffee
½ cup	whole hazelnuts
1 medium	whole egg
1 medium	egg white
⅓ cup	castor sugar
3 tablespoons	castor sugar[S] or granular Splenda® [ES]
½ teaspoon	vanilla essence

1. Preheat the oven to 180°C (160°C fan). Lightly grease 2 oven trays.
2. Combine the flour, baking powder, coffee and nuts. Beat the whole egg and egg white with the first measure of sugar, second measure of sugar or Splenda® and the essence until thick and foamy. Mix through the dry ingredients.
3. Roll into a 5 cm diameter log. Place on an oven tray and bake for 20 minutes. Remove from the oven and leave until cold. Slice into thin slices with a serrated knife.
4. Place on a lightly greased or lined oven tray. Bake at 150°C (130°C fan) for 15 – 20 minutes until slightly browned and crisp. Cool and then store in an airtight container. Will keep up to 4 weeks.

Nutrition Information (per serve)

Energy: 212 kj (51 cal) Carbohydrate: 7 g Fibre: 0.4 g Total fat: 1.9 g Saturated fat: 0.2 g Sodium: 14 mg GI: Medium

Apricot Chewy Cookies

These are like an Anzac biscuit without all the coconut and with the addition of dried apricots and walnuts. They need to be stored in an airtight container to stop them from softening.

12 serves	24 serves	ingredients
6	12	dried apricots
60 grams	125 grams	(70% fat) polyunsaturated margarine
1 tablespoon	2 tablespoons	golden syrup
½ teaspoon	1 teaspoon	baking soda
1½ tablespoons	3 tablespoons	low fat milk
½ cup	1 cup	plain flour
4 dessertspoons	⅓ cup	lightly packed brown sugar
4 dessertspoons	⅓ cup	granular Splenda® ES or castor sugarS
½ tablespoon	1 tablespoon	desiccated coconut
¾ cup	1½ cups	rolled oats
2 tablespoons	¼ cup	chopped walnuts

1. Preheat the oven to 180°C (160°C fan). Lightly grease 1 – 2 oven trays.
2. Dice the apricots into small cubes.
3. Combine the apricots, margarine and syrup in a pan. Heat over a low heat until the margarine melts. Remove from the heat.
4. Dissolve the soda in the milk. Add to the apricot mixture and leave to cool.
5. Combine the flour, brown sugar, Splenda® or castor sugar, coconut, oats and walnuts. Add the apricot mixture and mix well. The mixture should be quite wet.
6. Roll into 12 balls (12 serves) or 24 balls (24 serves) and place on the oven trays. Place a 7 cm square cutter over a biscuit and flatten to fit this. Remove and repeat with the remaining biscuits.
7. Bake for 10 – 15 minutes until cooked and browned. Leave to sit for 5 minutes before placing on a cooling rack. When cold place in an airtight container. Will keep 2 weeks.

Nutrition Information (per serve)

Energy: 399 kj (95 cal)   Carbohydrate: 11 g   Fibre: 1.0 g   Total fat: 4.9 g   Saturated fat: 1.1 g   Sodium: 54 mg   GI: Medium

Muesli Slice

Muesli slices and bars are not always healthy as they often contain a lot of butter and sugar or honey. This one is healthy, and it is packed with nuts and fruits.

24 serves	ingredients
1 cup	wholemeal flour
1 cup	rolled oats
2 tablespoons	desiccated coconut
1 tablespoon	baking powder
1 teaspoon	ground cinnamon
¼ cup	chopped walnuts
¼ cup	chopped hazelnuts
¼ cup	sultanas
¼ cup	lightly packed brown sugar
¼ cup	castor sugar[S] or granular Splenda® [ES]
2 tablespoons	sunflower seeds
½ cup	dried apricots
⅓ cup	dried prunes
1 medium	eating apple
75 grams	reduced fat (<56% fat) polyunsaturated margarine
2 tablespoons	no added sugar apple juice concentrate
2 teaspoons	grated lemon rind
1 medium	whole egg
½ cup	low fat plain unsweetened yoghurt

1. Preheat the oven to 180°C (160°C fan). Line a 24 cm square cake tin with baking paper.
2. Combine the flour, oats, coconut, baking powder, cinnamon, nuts, sultanas, brown sugar, castor sugar or Splenda® and sunflower seeds.
3. Dice the apricots and prunes into small cubes. Leaving the skin on the apple, core then grate.
4. Melt the margarine. Add the apricots, prunes, grated apple, juice, rind, egg and yoghurt. Stir through the dry ingredients and mix well.
5. Press into the tin. Bake for 20 – 25 minutes or until cooked.
6. When cool cut into 24 (6 x 4 cm) slices.
7. Keep in an airtight container in a cool place. Will keep 3 days.

Nutrition Information (per serve)

Energy: 425 kj (102 cal) Carbohydrate: 12 g Fibre: 1.7 g Total fat: 4.7 g Saturated fat: 1.0 g Sodium: 79 mg GI: Low

Fruit Crumble Slice

Sweeteners can not totally replace sugar, as they are unable to tenderise or brown baked products. Using a combination of sugar and a sweetener is a way of not compromising the texture, flavour and appearance.

20 serves	ingredients	20 serves	ingredients
	Base and Topping:		Filling:
1 cup	wholemeal flour	1 medium	eating apple
½ cup	plain flour	1 cup	sultanas
1 cup	rolled oats	½ cup	dried currants
⅓ cup	wheat bran	½ cup	dried dates
2 teaspoons	baking powder	1 teaspoon	ground cinnamon
½ cup	lightly packed brown sugar	1 teaspoon	grated lemon rind
¼ cup	equivalent sweetener[ES] or castor sugar[S]	1 tablespoon	lemon juice
		1½ cups	no added sugar apple juice
125 grams	reduced fat (<56% fat) polyunsaturated margarine	1 tablespoon	cornflour
3 tablespoons	low fat natural yoghurt		
½ cup	chopped walnuts		

1. Preheat the oven to 180°C (160°C fan). Line a 20 x 25 cm tin with baking paper.
2. **Base and Topping:** Combine the flours, oats, bran, baking powder, brown sugar and sweetener or castor sugar. Melt the margarine and mix through the dry ingredients, along with the yoghurt.
3. **Filling:** Leaving the skin on the apple, core then grate. Place in a pan with the sultanas, currants, dates, cinnamon, rind, lemon and apple juices. Bring to the boil then simmer for 10 minutes.
4. Mix the cornflour with a little water to form a smooth paste. Add to the fruit and stir over a low heat until thick. Leave to cool.
5. **Assembling:** Press two thirds of the base and topping mixture into the tin. Spread over the fruit mixture. Crumble over the remaining mixture and the walnuts.
6. Bake for 15 – 20 minutes or until cooked. When cool cut into 20 (5 x 4 cm) slices.
7. Keep in an airtight container in a cool place. Will keep 3 days.

Nutrition Information (per serve)

Energy: 721 kj (172 cal) Carbohydrate: 28 g Fibre: 2.3 g Total fat: 5.3 g Saturated fat: 0.7 g Sodium: 85 mg GI: Medium

Spicy Apple & Currant Slice

I have found that you cannot totally eliminate the sugar in baked products without compromising the taste, texture and look of a product. A small amount of sugar in the diet is acceptable, even for most people with diabetes.

16 serves	ingredients
1 cup	plain flour
2 teaspoons	baking powder
½ teaspoon	baking soda
2 teaspoons	ground mixed spice
½ cup	oat bran
½ cup	ground almonds
½ cup	dried currants
100 grams	reduced fat (<56% fat) polyunsaturated margarine
¼ cup	castor sugar
¼ cup	granular Splenda® ES or castor sugarS
2 teaspoons	grated lemon rind
1 medium	whole egg
1 medium	egg white
1 x 150 ml pottle	low fat plain unsweetened natural yoghurt
2 tablespoons	low fat milk
½ x 400 gram can	diced apple, in natural juice
Topping 16	whole walnuts or pecans

1   Preheat the oven to 180°C (160°C fan). Line a 20 cm square tin with baking paper.
2   Sift the flour, baking powder, soda and spice. Add the oat bran, almonds and currants.
3   Beat the margarine with the two measures of sugar or the first measure of sugar and the Splenda® and rind until light and fluffy. Continue beating while adding the eggs.
4   Stir in the yoghurt, milk and apple. Fold through the dried ingredients. Do not over mix.
5   Spread the mixture in the tin and evenly space the walnuts or pecans on the top.
6   Bake for 35 – 40 minutes or until cooked.
7   Cool in the tin then slice into 16 squares (4 x 4 cm). Keep in an airtight container in a cool place.
8   Lightly dust with icing sugar before serving. Will keep 3 days.

Nutrition Information (per serve)
Energy: 693 kj (166 cal)   Carbohydrate: 17 g   Fibre: 1.4 g   Total fat: 8.7 g   Saturated fat: 1.1 g   Sodium: 139 mg   GI: Low

Pear & Ginger Muesli Cake

Fat and sugar have many roles in baked products, one of them being to help tenderise. Buttermilk and yoghurt are great substitutes as they have a similar effect but are low in fat and sugar.

14 serves	ingredients
1½ cups	plain flour
1 teaspoon	ground ginger
1 teaspoon	ground cinnamon
½ teaspoon	ground cloves
1 teaspoon	baking soda
3 teaspoons	baking powder
½ cup	oat bran
2½ cups	unsweetened and untoasted muesli
2 medium	egg yolks
1 cup	buttermilk
1 x 410 gram can	pears, in natural juice
125 grams	reduced fat (<56% fat) polyunsaturated margarine
2 tablespoons	golden syrup
⅓ cup	lightly packed brown sugar
⅓ cup	granular Splenda® ES or castor sugarS
3 medium	egg whites
Topping 1	fresh eating pear

1. Preheat the oven to 180°C (160°C fan). Line the base of a 20 cm round tin with baking paper and lightly grease the sides.
2. Sift the flour, spices, soda and baking powder. Add the oat bran and muesli. Beat the egg yolks with the buttermilk. Drain and chop the canned pears into small chunks.
3. Beat the margarine, syrup, brown sugar and Splenda® or castor sugar until creamed.
4. Beat the egg whites until thick and foamy. Add the dry ingredients, egg yolk mixture, pears, and egg whites to the creamed mixture. Fold through gently and do not over mix.
5. Place in the tin and level. Leaving the skin on the pear, core and slice into slivers. Layer on the top of the cake. Bake for 1 – 1¼ hours or until cooked. Leave in the tin for 10 minutes then place on a cooling rack until cold. Store in an airtight container in a cool place.
6. It is best eaten warm, on the day of making.

Nutrition Information (per serve)

Energy: 883 kj (211 cal)   Carbohydrate: 34 g   Fibre: 3.7 g   Total fat: 6.2 g   Saturated fat: 1.1 g   Sodium: 250 mg   GI: Low

Apricot & Orange Mediterranean Cake

I had many failed attempts at trying to make an orange cake. This recipe was the last chance this cake had before I was going to cull it. It worked really well – and it got rave reviews.

10 serves	ingredients	10 serves	ingredients
½ cup	dried apricots	2 tablespoons	icing sugar
½ cup	no added sugar orange juice	75 grams	reduced fat (<56% fat) polyunsaturated margarine
1 medium	orange		
1 cup	plain flour	¼ cup	castor sugar
2 tablespoons	custard powder	½ cup	granular Splenda® ES or castor sugarˢ
4 teaspoons	baking powder		
½ cup	ground almonds	2 medium	egg yolks
½ cup	oat bran	1 cup	buttermilk
¾ cup	(8% fat) ricotta	4 medium	egg whites
1 teaspoon	grated orange rind		

1   Preheat the oven to 180°C (160°C fan). Line the base of a 20 cm round cake tin with baking paper and lightly grease the sides.
2   Slice the apricots into small slivers. Bring the orange juice to the boil and then pour over the apricots.
3   Place the whole orange, in a saucepan, and cover with water. Bring to the boil and then simmer for 20 minutes. Drain the water. Place the orange in a food processor and process until smooth. Cool.
4   Sift the flour, custard powder and baking powder. Add the almonds and oat bran.
5   Combine half of the apricots and juice with the ricotta, rind and icing sugar.
6   Cream the margarine, the first measure of sugar, Splenda® or the second measure of sugar and egg yolks until creamy. Add the processed orange.
7   Gently mix through the remaining apricots, dry ingredients and the buttermilk.
8   Beat the egg whites until thick and foamy. Fold through gently.
9   Place one half of the mixture into the tin and level. Dot over the ricotta mixture, leaving a 2 cm border around the outside of the cake. Place the remaining cake batter gently on the top and spread to cover the ricotta.
10   Bake for 60 – 70 minutes or until cooked. If the cake is browning too quickly during cooking, cover with aluminium foil. Remove from the oven and leave in the tin for 10 minutes. Place on a cooling rack until cool.
11   It is best eaten on the day of making. Lightly dust with icing sugar before serving.

Nutrition Information (per serve)

Energy: 1010 kj (242 cal)   Carbohydrate: 30 g   Fibre: 1.9 g   Total fat: 9.7 g   Saturated fat: 2.2 g   Sodium: 279 mg   GI: Low

Chocolate Cake or Black Forest Gateau

The prunes, which are high in fibre, provide a richness and moistness to this cake – and you can't taste them!

10 – 12 serves	ingredients	10 – 12 serves	ingredients
250 grams	dried prunes	2 medium	egg yolks
1¼ cups	no added sugar apple juice	⅔ cup	buttermilk
4 teaspoons	instant coffee	2 tablespoons	Irish Cream or brandy
¼ cup	castor sugar		Chocolate Cake Icing:
½ cup	granular Splenda® ES or sugarS	1 sachet	Weight Watchers™ chocolate
1 tablespoon	vegetable oil		mousse
1 teaspoon	baking soda	1 cup	low fat (5%) cream cheese
⅓ cup	cocoa		Gateau Filling:
¾ cup	plain flour	2 sachets	Weight Watchers™ chocolate
3 teaspoons	baking powder		mousse
¾ cup	ground almonds	1 cup	fresh berries or canned
4 medium	egg whites		cherries

1 Preheat the oven to 170°C (150°C fan). Line the base of a 20 cm round cake tin with baking paper and lightly grease the sides.

2 Chop the prunes into small pieces. Bring the prunes and juice to the boil then simmer for 5 minutes.

3 Mix through the coffee, sugar/Splenda®, oil and soda. Cool.

4 Sift the cocoa, flour and baking powder. Add the ground almonds.

5 Beat the egg whites until thick and foamy. Gently fold the dry ingredients, egg whites, egg yolks, buttermilk and liqueur or brandy through the prune mixture. Do not over mix.

6 Place into the tin. Cover with aluminium foil. Bake for 1 – 1¼ hours or until cooked.

7 Leave in the tin for 10 minutes then place on a cooling rack until cold.

8 **Chocolate Cake Icing:** Beat the mousse with the cream cheese until smooth. Spread quickly over the top of the cake. Refrigerate. Slice the cake into 10 pieces.

9 **Gateau Filling:** Slice the cake into 3 even pieces horizontally. Make up one mousse according to the instructions on the packet. Spread quickly onto the bottom cake layer. Place half of the berries over the mousse and then place the middle layer of cake on top. Repeat with the remaining mousse, berries and cake.

10 Decorate the top with berries, edible flowers and a dusting of icing sugar and slice into 12 pieces.

Nutrition Information (per serve) Black Forest Gateau
Energy: 921 kj (220 cal) Carbohydrate: 31 g Fibre: 2.1 g Total fat: 7.3 g Saturated fat: 1.8 g Sodium: 222 mg GI: Low

Black Forest Gateau

christmas

Truffles pg 166

Fresh Cherries

Christmas Fruit Mince Pies pg 164

Christmas is as much about food as it is about presents and family get togethers. At this time of the year there is often so much food around that we are tempted to overeat. Overeating doesn't feel good – and it ruins the enjoyment of the food that has been eaten. If you have to taste everything on offer – keep the portions small.

Don't forget there are lots of kilojoules in alcohol and standard soft drinks – space alcohol out with diet drinks or water. NOSH recipes will help you get a taste of Christmas – and yummy at that, with less fat, sugar and kilojoules.

Keep festive eating for Christmas Day and then enjoy the leftovers on Boxing Day. For the rest of the holiday season enjoy the abundance of fresh seasonal berry and stone fruits, barbecues (healthy ones!) and salads.

Christmas Pudding

This is a really easy Christmas pudding to make. Most traditional Christmas puddings – but not this one, are made with suet which is high in saturated fat!

10 serves	ingredients	10 serves	ingredients
1 medium	eating apple	½ cup	sultanas
½ cup	no added sugar apple juice	½ cup	dried currants
2 tablespoons	treacle	¼ cup	raisins
1 tablespoon	vegetable oil	1 medium	whole egg
¼ cup	dried figs	½ cup	plain flour
¼ cup	dried apricots	½ cup	wholemeal flour
½ teaspoon	baking soda	½ teaspoon	ground cinnamon
½ cup	low fat milk	½ teaspoon	ground mixed spice
1 teaspoon	grated orange rind	⅛ teaspoon	ground cloves
1 teaspoon	grated lemon rind	1 teaspoon	baking powder

1. Lightly grease a 4 cup ovenproof bowl.
2. Leaving the skin on the apple, core and dice. Place in a pan with the juice and cook until soft. Take off the heat and add the treacle and oil. Leave to cool.
3. Slice the figs and apricots into small pieces. Dissolve the soda in the milk. Combine all the ingredients. Place in the greased bowl and cover first with baking paper then aluminium foil.
4. Place in a large saucepan. Add warm water until it is three quarters of the way up the side of the bowl. The water may need to be topped up during cooking.
5. Bring to the boil then simmer for 1¾ – 2 hours or until cooked. Leave to cool.
6. When cold, place in an airtight container in the refrigerator or freezer. Will keep for 1 week refrigerated, or 1 – 2 months frozen. If frozen, defrost before reheating. Reheat in the microwave on low for 10 – 15 minutes or in a water bath for 1 hour or until heated through.

Nutrition Information (per serve)
Energy: 697 kj (167 cal) Carbohydrate: 33 g Fibre: 2.2 g Total fat: 2.5 g Saturated fat: 0.5 g Sodium: 124 mg GI: Medium

Last Minute Christmas Cake

This is a great last minute cake which is really moist. The coffee and cocoa make this cake a darker colour, like a traditional Christmas cake, without having any effect on the flavour.

50 serves	ingredients	50 serves	ingredients
1 medium	eating apple	1 tablespoon	instant coffee
¾ cup	dried prunes	1 teaspoon	baking soda
¾ cup	dried apricots	3 medium	whole eggs
1 tablespoon	grated orange rind	70 gram packet	walnut pieces
2 teaspoons	grated lemon rind	1 cup	plain flour
1½ cups	sultanas	1 cup	wholemeal flour
½ cup	raisins	1 teaspoon	baking powder
1 cup	dried currants	1 tablespoon	cocoa
1 x 225 gram can	crushed pineapple, in natural juice	1½ teaspoons	ground cinnamon
		1½ teaspoons	ground mixed spice
1½ cups	no added sugar old fashioned apple juice	Topping:	whole blanched almonds
		70 g packet	whole blanched almonds
⅓ cup	brandy	70 g packet	walnut halves
150 grams	reduced fat (<56% fat) polyunsaturated margarine	5	halved red and green glace cherries

1. Preheat the oven to 140°C (120°C fan). Line the base and sides of a 20 cm tin with tinfoil and baking paper.
2. Leaving the skin on the apple, core and dice finely. Slice the prunes and apricots into small pieces.
3. Place the apple, prunes, apricots, rinds, sultanas, raisins, currants, pineapple and juice, apple juice and brandy in a pan. Bring to the boil then simmer for 10 minutes. Take off the heat, add the margarine and stir until melted. Add the coffee and soda and leave to cool.
4. Lightly beat the eggs. Add the eggs, first measure of walnuts and the dry ingredients to the fruit mixture. Stir until well combined.
5. Place in the tin and level. Place a row of almonds around the outside of the cake, then a row of walnut halves and then the cherries, alternating the colours.
6. Bake for 2½ – 3 hours or until cooked. If the cake is browning too quickly during cooking, cover with foil.
7. Leave in the tin to cool. When cold, place in an airtight container in the refrigerator or freezer. Will keep for 4 weeks refrigerated, or 2 months frozen.

Nutrition Information (per serve)

Energy: 385 kj (92 cal) Carbohydrate: 15 g Fibre: 1.1 g Total fat: 2.8 g Saturated fat: 0.5 g Sodium: 49 mg GI: Low

Christmas Fruit Mince Filo Cigars

Christmas Fruit Mincemeat

It's not hard to make your own Christmas mincemeat. There is no need to add any sugar as the fruit will provide enough sweetness. Leave for at least 3 – 4 days, before using, so that the flavours can develop.

2 cups	ingredients
1 medium	eating apple
⅓ cup	dried prunes
⅓ cup	dried apricots
1 cup	sultanas
⅓ cup	dried currants
1 teaspoon	grated lemon rind
1 teaspoon	grated orange rind
½ teaspoon	ground cinnamon
½ teaspoon	ground mixed spice
¼ teaspoon	ground cloves
¼ – ½ cup	brandy or sherry

1. Leaving the skin on the apple, core and slice. Slice the prunes and apricots into smaller pieces.
2. Place the apple, prunes, apricots, half of the sultanas and currants, rinds, spices and brandy or sherry into a food processor.
3. Process until smooth. Stir through the remaining sultanas and currants.
4. Place in sterilised jars in the refrigerator. Will keep for 1 month.

Nutrition Information (per teaspoon)

Energy: 42 kj (10 cal) Carbohydrate: 2 g Fibre: 0.2 g Total fat: 0.02 g Saturated fat: 0 g
Sodium: 1 mg GI: Low GF* Use GF spices.

Christmas Fruit Mince Filo Cigars

These look really cool and you don't have to make the pastry. Filo is a low fat pastry provided that you do not brush it too heavily with fat.

12 serves	ingredients
4 tablespoons	reduced fat (<56% fat) polyunsaturated margarine
12 sheets	filo pastry
1 cup	Christmas fruit mincemeat (as above)

1. Preheat the oven to 190°C (170°C fan). Line an oven tray with baking paper. Melt the margarine.
2. Take 1 sheet of the filo at a time. Fold both of the edges on the long sides into the middle and lightly brush with the margarine.
3. Place 4 teaspoons of the mincemeat, in a 1 cm roll, along one of the short edges of the pastry, leaving a 1 cm gap at each end.
4. Roll up and place on the tray. Brush with margarine. Repeat the process.
5. Bake for 15 minutes or until browned. Cool and store in an airtight tin in a cool place. Serve reheated for 5 minutes in a hot oven and lightly dusted with icing sugar.

Nutrition Information (per serve)

Energy: 414 kj (99 cal) Carbohydrate: 16 g Fibre: 0.9 g Total fat: 2.7 g Saturated fat: 0.4 g
Sodium: 117 mg GI: Low

Christmas Fruit Mince Pies

These can be made a couple of days before eating, at the longest, so that the pastry doesn't go too soft. Make them into mouthfuls – this way, on Christmas Day, you can have a small amount of everything without overindulging. Reheating prior to serving will freshen them up.

18 serves	ingredients
3 tablespoons	(70% fat) polyunsaturated margarine
1 tablespoon	icing sugar
2 teaspoons	custard powder
¾ cup	plain flour
1 teaspoon	baking powder
1 tablespoon	ground almonds
¼ cup	low fat milk
1 cup	Christmas fruit mincemeat (page 163)

1. In a food processor or mixer place the margarine, icing sugar, custard powder, flour, baking powder and almonds. Mix until the mixture resembles fine breadcrumbs.
2. Add the milk until the mixture is soft and combined.
3. Wrap in cling film and refrigerate for at least 30 minutes.
4. Preheat the oven to 180°C (160°C fan). Lightly grease 18 mini muffin tins.
5. Roll the pastry out thinly. Cut out circles to fit the base and sides of the muffin tins. Place into the tins. Add the fruit mince up to the top of the pastry.
6. Cut out of the remaining pastry, small stars or Christmas trees. Place one shape on top of each pie.
7. Bake for 15 minutes until cooked and browned.
8. Cool. Store in an airtight container in the refrigerator. Lightly dust with icing sugar before serving.
9. Best eaten within a couple of days or freeze for up to 2 weeks. If frozen, defrost and then reheat in the oven.

Nutrition Information (per serve)

Energy: 280 kj (67 cal)   Carbohydrate: 11 g   Fibre: 0.5 g   Total fat: 2.1 g   Saturated fat: 0.4 g   Sodium: 34 mg   GI: Medium

Truffles

These delicious truffles are not sickly sweet. The chocolate cake is low in fat and is also gluten free. It can be substituted with any uniced chocolate cake that has less than 10% fat.

	30 serves	ingredients
	½ cup	dried prunes
	½ cup	dried figs
	¼ cup	hot strong espresso or plunger coffee
or	1 tablespoon	instant coffee
and	¼ cup	hot water
	3 tablespoons	Irish Cream liqueur
	75 grams	dark chocolate
	350 grams	4 Ever Free® Chocolate and Raisin Cake
	as required	chopped pistachios, cocoa, flaked or ground almonds

1. Slice the prunes and figs into small pieces. Place in a bowl and pour over the hot coffee and liqueur. Sit covered at room temperature for 30 minutes.
2. Melt the chocolate over a low heat.
3. Crumble the cake.
4. Mix the prune and fig mixture through the crumbled cake.
5. Add the melted chocolate and stir through.
6. Roll into small balls and then coat in nuts or cocoa. Refrigerate for at least 2 hours before eating.
7. Store in an airtight container in the refrigerator. Will keep for 1 week.

Nutrition Information (per serve)

Energy: 339 kj (81 cal) Carbohydrate: 12 g Fibre: 0.5 g Total fat: 3.1 g Saturated fat: 0.6 g Sodium: 5 mg GI: Low
GF* No modifications needed. The cake is gluten free.

preserves, spreads & sauces

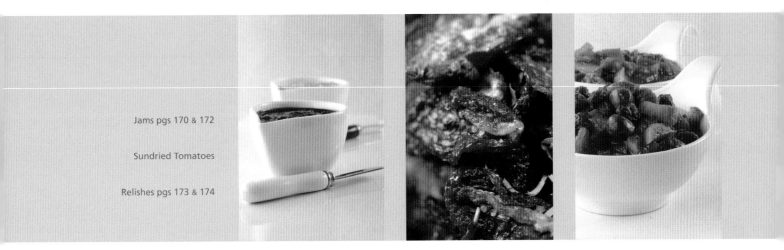

Jams pgs 170 & 172

Sundried Tomatoes

Relishes pgs 173 & 174

It might be old fashioned – but making homemade preserves is becoming a new trend. Preserves are a way of adding flavour to a meal without lots of sugar, fat, salt and kilojoules.

There are some key principles to preserving without large amounts of sugar. Use only fruit or vegetables that are well ripened, but not over ripe. The jams are cooked when they have become the consistency of syrup. The preserves should be placed into small 250 gram (1 cup) or smaller jars with metal screw lids. The jars and lids must be thoroughly cleaned, dried and then sterilised in the oven, at 120°C (100°C fan), for at least 30 minutes. The preserves must be placed hot, into hot jars, and then sealed. Leave until cold, then refrigerate. Properly sealed preserves should last 4 months. Once opened, keep refrigerated and seal after use. Use clean utensils for serving to avoid contamination which will hasten the spoiling process.

Savoury spreads and sauces are often high in fat. The cheese spread is a great way to make cheese go further and the processed cheese slices add a creaminess with less fat.

Cheese Spread

This is a good way of extending and adding more flavour to cheese. To make yummy cheese rolls, spread it onto thin slices of grainy bread and roll up. Spray lightly with oil and grill until browned and heated through.

1 – 1½ cups		ingredients
	8	reduced fat processed cheese slices
	200 ml	reduced fat evaporated milk
	2 teaspoons	French onion soup powder
and	2 tablespoons	chopped spring onions
	2 tablespoons	chopped red pepper
or	2 tablespoons	crushed pineapple
	2 tablespoons	chopped lean ham

1. Combine the cheese, milk, soup powder and flavourings together in a double boiler or in a microwave proof bowl.
2. If cooking in a double boiler, cook over a medium heat. If cooking in the microwave, cook on low. Stir often, until the cheese has melted. Leave to cool.
3. Place in a sterilised jar with a lid and refrigerate. Will keep for 2 weeks.

Nutrition Information (per teaspoon) plain flavour

Energy: 48 kj (11 cal)   Carbohydrate: 0.7 g   Fibre: 0.01 g   Total fat: 0.5 g   Saturated fat: 0.3 g   Sodium: 64 mg   GI: Low   GF* Use GF cheese slices, evaporated milk and soup powder.

Quick Cheese Sauce

Most hard cheeses are high in fat. Keep the quantity of cheese that you eat small, and where possible choose lower fat varieties like cottage cheese. Edam cheese is not a low fat cheese, but it does contain less fat than most hard cheeses.

1 cup	ingredients
¾ cup	low fat milk
½ teaspoon	French onion soup powder
3	reduced fat processed cheese slices
2 teaspoons	cornflour
2 teaspoons	low fat milk

1. Place the first measure of the milk and the soup powder into a pan and heat over a low heat until nearly boiling.
2. Add the cheese, stirring continuously, over a low heat until the cheese melts.
3. Dissolve the cornflour in the remaining milk. Add to the sauce and cook until thickened.
4. Serve immediately.

Nutrition Information (per ¼ cup)

Energy: 280 kj (67 cal)   Carbohydrate: 5 g   Fibre: 0.02 g   Total fat: 1.9 g   Saturated fat: 1.0 g   Sodium: 309 mg   GI: Low   GF* Use GF cheese slices, soup powder and cornflour.

Plum Jam

Plums tend to be quite tart when cooked, so this jam needs the addition of a sweetener on top of the apple juice to give it a satisfactory sweetness.

1 cup	2 cups	ingredients
13 (650 grams)	26 (1.3 kilograms)	fresh eating plums
⅔ cup	1⅓ cups	no added sugar apple juice concentrate
to taste	to taste	sweetener[ES]

1. Remove the stones from the plums. Place the plums and the juice in a pan.
2. Bring to the boil and simmer, stirring often, until thickened (40 – 50 minutes).
3. Add the sweetener to taste and stir until dissolved.
4. Pour into small, hot sterilised jars and seal. Leave to cool.
5. Keep in the refrigerator. Will last 2 – 3 weeks when opened.

Nutrition Information (per teaspoon)
Energy: 60 kj (14 cal) **Carbohydrate:** 3.2 g **Fibre:** 0.2 g
Total fat: 0.8 g **Saturated fat:** 0.01 g **Sodium:** 0.7 mg
GI: Low **GF*** No modifications needed.

Fruit Salad Jam

The great thing about this jam is that you can make it all year round as the fruits are not seasonal. I'm not a cooked banana fan but adding banana to this fruit combination adds a delicious dimension.

2 cups	4 cups	ingredients
1 cup (125 grams)	2 cups (250 grams)	dried apricots
1½ cups	3 cups	no added sugar orange juice
½ cup	1 cup	crushed pineapple, in natural juice
¼ cup	½ cup	passionfruit dessert topping or pulp
1 medium	2 medium	banana/s

1. Slice the apricots into small pieces. Soak in the juice overnight.
2. Combine the apricots and pineapple, including the juice, in a pan. Simmer for 15 minutes then add the passionfruit topping.
3. Slice the banana/s and add. Bring to the boil and simmer, stirring often, until the mixture thickens (20 – 30 minutes).
4. Pour into small, sterilised jars and seal. Leave to cool.
5. Keep in the refrigerator. Will last 5 – 6 weeks when opened.

Nutrition Information (per teaspoon)
Energy: 27 kj (6 cal) **Fibre:** 0.2 g **Carbohydrate:** 1.5 g
Total fat: 0.02 g **Saturated fat:** 0 g **Sodium:** 0.8 mg
GI: Low **GF*** Use GF passionfruit topping.

Boysenberry Jam pg 172 (front) and Fruit Salad Jam (back)

Boysenberry Jam

The key to making nice jams, without adding sucrose (white sugar), is to use a concentrated fruit juice and to cook the fruit until it thickens. This way the flavour and texture are much more like ordinary jams.

1 cup	2 cups	ingredients
2 cups (250 grams)	4 cups (500 grams)	fresh or frozen boysenberries
½ cup	1 cup	no added sugar concentrated apple juice
1 tablespoon	2 tablespoons	lemon juice

1. Place the boysenberries in a pan with the apple and lemon juices. Bring to the boil and simmer, stirring frequently, until thickened (20 – 30 minutes).
2. Pour into small, hot sterilised jars and seal. Leave to cool.
3. Keep in the refrigerator. Will last 2 – 3 weeks when opened.

Nutrition Information (per teaspoon)

Energy: 29 kj (7 cal) **Carbohydrate:** 1.4 g **Fibre:** 0.01 g
Total fat: 0.04 g **Saturated fat:** 0 g **Sodium:** 0.3 mg
GI: Low **GF*** No modifications needed.

Apricot Jam

These jams are much more flavoursome than standard jams. The fruit flavour is not diluted by great amounts of sugar. Use ripe fruits, as these will give a greater natural sweetness to the jams.

1 cup	2 cups	ingredients
5 (250 grams)	10 (500 grams)	fresh apricots
¼ cup	½ cup	no added sugar apple juice concentrate

1. Remove the stones and chop the apricots into smaller pieces.
2. Place in a pan and add the juice. Bring to the boil and simmer, stirring often, until thickened (30 – 40 minutes).
3. Pour into small, hot sterilised jars and seal. Leave to cool.
4. Keep in the refrigerator. Will last 2 – 3 weeks when opened.

Nutrition Information (per teaspoon)

Energy: 20 kj (5 cal) **Carbohydrate:** 1 g **Fibre:** 0.05 g
Total fat: 0.02 g **Saturated fat:** 0 g **Sodium:** 0.2 mg
GI: Low **GF*** No modifications needed.

Tomato Relish

Low sugar relishes, chutneys and sauces, made with large quantities of vinegar, will last a lot longer than jams made without sugar. Vinegar acts as a preservative.

2 – 2½ cups	4 – 5 cups	ingredients
3 (375 grams)	6 (750 grams)	tomatoes
1 medium	2 medium	onion/s
1 medium	2 medium	eating apple/s
½ cup	1 cup	sultanas
¾ cup	1½ cups	cider vinegar
¼ cup	½ cup	no added sugar apple juice concentrate
½ teaspoon	1 teaspoon	iodised salt
1 teaspoon	2 teaspoons	mustard powder
¼ teaspoon	½ teaspoon	curry powder
pinch	¼ teaspoon	cayenne pepper
pinch	¼ teaspoon	ground cloves
1 teaspoon	2 teaspoons	cornflour
1 teaspoon	2 teaspoons	cold water

1   Chop the tomatoes into quarters.
2   Peel and slice the onion/s finely. Leaving the skin on the apple/s, core and finely dice.
3   Place all the ingredients in a pan except the cornflour and the water.
4   Bring to the boil and simmer, stirring often, for 1 hour.
5   Mix the cornflour with the water until smooth. Stir through until a desired thickness is achieved.
    Cook for a further 5 minutes without stirring.
6   Place in hot sterilised jars and seal. Leave to cool.
7   Keep in the refrigerator.
8   Will last up to 6 weeks when opened.

Nutrition Information (per teaspoon)

Energy: 18 kj (4 cal)   Carbohydrate: 0.9 g   Fibre: 0.1 g   Total fat: 0.02 g   Saturated fat: 0 g   Sodium: 9.7 mg   GI: Low
GF* Use GF mustard, curry powder and cornflour.

Fruit Chutney

This chutney is full of flavour and chunks of fruit. It is great served with cold meats and quiches.

2 – 2½ cups	4 – 5 cups	ingredients
1 medium	2 medium	eating apple/s
½ medium	1 medium	onion
⅓ cup	⅔ cup	dried apricots
⅓ cup	⅔ cup	dried dates
¼ cup	½ cup	dried figs
⅓ cup	⅔ cup	black seedless grapes
⅓ cup	⅔ cup	sultanas
¼ cup	½ cup	medium white wine
½ cup	1 cup	cold water
1	2	clove/s
½ teaspoon	1 teaspoon	crushed garlic
½ teaspoon	1 teaspoon	crushed ginger
pinch teaspoon	¼ teaspoon	chilli powder
½	1	cinnamon stick
½ cup	1 cup	no added sugar orange juice

1. Leaving the skin on the apple/s, core and finely dice. Finely dice the onion, apricots, dates and figs.
2. Place all the ingredients in a pan. Bring to the boil then simmer, stirring often, for 30 – 40 minutes until thick. Remove the clove/s and cinnamon stick.
3. Pour into small, hot sterilised jars and seal. Leave to cool.
4. Keep in the refrigerator.
5. Will last 2 – 3 weeks when opened.

Nutrition Information (per teaspoon)

Energy: 34 kj (8 cal) Carbohydrate: 1.8 g Fibre: 0.1 g Total fat: 0.02 g Saturated fat: 0 g Sodium: 0.7 mg GI: Medium
GF* Use GF chilli powder.

Fruit Chutney (front) and Tomato Relish pg 173 (back)

index

index